BECOMING A 401(K) MILLIONAIRE

BECOMING A 401(K) MILLIONAIRE

MAKING THE MOST OF YOUR COMPANY RETIREMENT PLAN

By Dr. Peter Fisher

© 2024 by Dr. Peter Fisher

All rights reserved. This book or any portion thereof may not be reproduced or used in any manner whatsoever without the express written permission of the publisher except for the use of brief quotations in a book review.

ISBN: 9798344084152

CONTENTS

Foreword · vii
Acknowledgments · ix
Introduction · xi

Part I: Mapping the Retirement Terrain and Securing Your Future · 1

    Chapter 1   From Small Beginnings to Big Dreams: The Power of a 401(k) · · · · · · · · · · · · · · · 3

    Chapter 2   Your Retirement Road Trip: From Point A to 401(k) · 13

    Chapter 3   Navigating Your Path to a Million-Dollar Retirement · 37

    Chapter 4   The Power of Starting Early: Budgeting and Saving for Retirement · · · · · · · · · · · 57

    Chapter 5   The Power of Small Decisions · · · · · · · · 75

    Chapter 6   The Power of the 401(k) and the Reality of Social Security · · · · · · · · · · · · · · · · · · 81

    Chapter 7   Flipping the Switch: From Saver to Spender in Retirement · 93

Part II: The Expanded Field of Retirement · · · · · · · · · 111

    Chapter 8   Tailored Retirement Solutions for Unique Situations · · · · · · · · · · · · · · · · · 113

Chapter 9   Financial Independence, Retire Early (FIRE):
A Radical Approach · · · · · · · · · · · · · · · · 127
Chapter 10 The Late Bloomers: It's Never Too Late
to Start Saving· 137
Chapter 11 Inspiring Savers: Real Stories of Hope · · 143

Part III: To Retire Is Human · **157**
Chapter 12 Market Timing, the News, and
Your Emotions· 159
Chapter 13 Mastering the Mind: Navigating Investor
Behavior and Emotions· · · · · · · · · · · · · 167
Chapter 14 From Pen to Platform: Bridging Theory
and Reality in Financial Literacy · · · · · · · 181
Chapter 15 The Grand Finale: Your Journey to
401(k) Success · · · · · · · · · · · · · · · · · · · 197

Author's Note · 205
Appendix· 207

FOREWORD

When Peter asked if I would write a foreword for his book, it was an easy yes. I've known Peter for nearly 20 years, and in that time, I've had the wonderful opportunity of not only being a client of Peter and his firm, Human Investing, but also a business coach and friend to him. Having written several books myself, I understand the time, effort, and expertise that goes into delivering useful advice and counsel to would-be readers.

Peter has done just that with this book. It's packed with practical steps to help everyday people save and invest—to prepare well financially for retirement. I've benefited from Peter's expertise, as he has counseled me on many of the same practical steps that appear in the book. He writes primarily for those who work for a company and invest in a retirement plan. The 401(k) plan is one of the greatest savings vehicles for all of us—but the ability to maximize the benefit of a retirement plan depends on one's ability to understand how and where to invest. We all need to see not only what a good 401(k) plan looks like but also how to steer clear of the bad ones.

Drawing on nearly 30 years of experience in the financial services industry, Peter and his team put their minds and hearts into what they do as retirement consultants. I know this firsthand, as they also work with my company's retirement plan, providing advice and counsel to my employees. I value Peter's approach and work so much that I've also introduced some of my clients to Peter. I've seen him help people of all socioeconomic levels in the same intentional way he does my employees and me.

The key takeaways he has put at the end of each chapter are practical, easy-to-understand action items for every retirement investor. He breaks it down and makes it real—we couldn't ask for more from the usually confusing world of 401(k) investing. I am confident that all who read this book and take advantage of its wisdom will be better off with a clearer understanding of retirement plan investing, how to begin, the truth of your 401(k) plan, why you should stick with it, and what retirement readiness means.

Sincerely,
Daniel Harkavy
Best-selling author
Founder and CEO, Building Champions
Executive coach

ACKNOWLEDGMENTS

To my family, I love you so much.
To our Lord, for the gift of life.

INTRODUCTION

It's been five years since the first edition of *Becoming a 401(k) Millionaire* hit the shelves. Shortly after its release, I embarked on a journey to sharpen my research skills by joining a doctoral program. Fast-forward to 2022, and with a shiny new doctorate in hand, I felt it was time to revisit and revise this book, armed with new insights into financial literacy and behavior.

The Big Question: What Is Retirement Anyway?

Though my sabbatical didn't exactly give me the ample time to edit the book I expected, I focused on adding new insights from my research. Specifically, I examined the current state of financial literacy while exploring contemporary investments such as cryptocurrency. Moreover, in this edition I explain the role of human behavior when investing—mobilizing what I learned in my doctoral-level studies. Yet I found myself still pondering a fundamental question: "What is retirement?"

As you likely gleaned from the title, this book aims to help you leverage a 401(k) plan while encouraging you to save, invest, and retire. But to what end? Specifically, does retirement have to follow the traditional script of the past 40 years?

According to the Center for Retirement Research at Boston College, the average retirement age for men is 64.7, and for women, 62.1.[1] But how do we define retirement today? Does it mean stopping work cold turkey? Or can it look different?

Let's begin by examining whether the mid-60s is really the right age to retire today. For most individuals, retiring around 65 makes sense, given that you are eligible to take Social Security at approximately that time. But even if the traditional retirement age of 65 or so might have made sense in the past, it's worth questioning if it's still the best choice for retirees today. For many, hitting the retirement milestone doesn't mean it's time to stop working altogether—in fact, many have found their 60s, 70s, and beyond some of the most rewarding times of their career.

Take Warren Buffett, for example. At 93, he's still at the helm of Berkshire Hathaway, making strategic investments and business decisions that influence markets worldwide. Remarkably, over 90 percent of Buffett's wealth has been accumulated since he turned 65.[2] Had Buffett retired at 65, the world would have missed nearly three decades of his

---

[1] Munnell, A. H. (2022). *How to think about recent trends in the average retirement age*. Issue in Brief 22-11. Center for Retirement Research at Boston College.

[2] Market Trading Essentials. (2022, March 31). *Warren Buffett has amassed over 90% of his wealth since he turned 65*. https://www.markettradingessentials.com/2022/03/warren-buffett-has-amassed-over-90-of-his-wealth-since-he-turned-65/

financial wisdom—not to mention his enormous financial gifts to nonprofits around the globe.

Or consider Peter Drucker, a renowned management consultant, educator, and author. Drucker continued to write and advise well into his 90s, significantly influencing modern management practices. His contributions in his later years continued to shape business thinking and practices globally—in addition to rewarding him financially.

Working in Retirement: More than Just Wealth Accumulation

Working in retirement can be about more than just accumulating wealth for yourself. It can be an opportunity to work and save for others—whether for your family, for your church, or to address global burdens such as hunger, education, and peace.

Consider the impact you can make by continuing to work and directing your efforts toward charitable causes. Many retirees find fulfillment in volunteering, mentoring, or even starting foundations to support causes they are passionate about. By doing so, they not only stay active and engaged but also contribute to the well-being of others. But what exactly does this choice look like? Let's look at a few real-world examples.

Linda's Legacy of Learning

Linda was a schoolteacher for 35 years before "retiring" at 62. Instead of fully stepping away from education, she chose to work part-time as a tutor. However, she didn't stop there. Linda used her skills to start a nonprofit organization that provides free tutoring and educational resources to underprivileged children in her community. Her efforts have helped hundreds of kids improve their academic performance and gain confidence.

By working in retirement, Linda soft-landed on a 30-plus-year career while making some "fun money," which allowed her to take less from her retirement savings. Importantly, she's using a lifetime's worth of experience with a new purpose and impacting the lives of many young students.

John's Journey with Building Homes

John, a former construction manager, retired at 65 but found himself missing the satisfaction of building and creating. Inspired by Jimmy Carter's example (discussed below), John joined a nonprofit and transitioned his time and expertise to help build homes for those in need. Over the past decade, John has helped construct over 50 houses, providing safe and affordable housing for countless families. His work keeps him physically active—and brings him immense joy and fulfillment as he sees the direct impact of his contributions. Plus, the small stipend he receives helps him minimize what he draws from his retirement accounts.

Maria's Mission for Health

Maria, a nurse who retired at 60, couldn't shake the feeling that she still had more to give. She combined her medical knowledge with her passion for helping by going to work at a local clinic. Additionally, Maria started a health education program for seniors, focusing on preventive care and healthy living. Her initiative has helped many older adults in her community lead healthier, more informed lives. Maria's postretirement work keeps her engaged and significantly improves the health and well-being of those she serves. In addition to blessing others, she has self-employment income from her health education business, which bolsters her retirement cash flow. Self-employment also allows for essential tax deductions and write-offs that help her retirement expenses go down.

David's Dedication to Global Causes

David spent his career in corporate finance, retiring at 58 with a comfortable nest egg. But instead of focusing solely on his own leisure, David chose to use his financial acumen to support global causes. He partnered with various NGOs, offering his expertise in financial management. As a for-hire CFO, David has helped raise millions of dollars for projects to reduce hunger and improve education in developing countries. His efforts have shown that working in retirement can extend far beyond personal gain, reaching those in dire need worldwide.

Ruth's Support for the Arts

Ruth, a successful graphic designer, retired at 54 but never lost her passion for the arts. She began volunteering at a local community center, teaching art classes to both children and adults. She also started a scholarship fund for aspiring young artists, funded by the sale of her own artwork. Her contributions have nurtured many individuals' talents and enriched her community's cultural fabric. Working in retirement allowed Ruth tax deductions, delayed drawdown of retirement accounts, and enabled a continuation of her creative pursuits while making a meaningful difference in the lives of others.

Iconic Examples

At another register, consider **Jimmy Carter**, the 39th President of the United States. After leaving the White House, Carter dedicated his life to humanitarian efforts, notably through the Carter Center. His work has focused on conflict resolution, disease eradication, and promoting democracy. Well into his 90s, Carter continued to build homes with Habitat for Humanity, showcasing that work in retirement can profoundly impact the lives of others.

Even after her successful career as a talk show host, **Oprah Winfrey** has dedicated much of her time and resources to educational initiatives through the Oprah Winfrey Leadership Academy for Girls in South Africa. Her postretirement efforts have provided educational opportunities to many underprivileged children.

The Personal Choice of Retirement

These individuals illustrate that many people find purpose and achieve significant milestones well past the typical retirement age. What can you take away from their stories? Rather than thinking about a set age, it might be more beneficial to consider what retirement means to you personally. For some, continuing to work brings financial gains, along with joy, fulfillment, and a sense of purpose.

For others, it's an opportunity to pursue new passions or spend time with family.

Ultimately, the decision to retire should be based on personal circumstances, health, and happiness. If you're passionate about your work and find it fulfilling, there's no reason to retire just because you've hit a certain age. On the flip side, retiring earlier or exploring new avenues might be the perfect choice if you're ready for a change and have the means to do so.

Whether it's continuing to work, starting a new venture, or dedicating time to hobbies and family, retirement can be a dynamic and evolving phase of life. **The key is to plan and save so that you can choose the right path for you, without being forced into a one-size-fits-all model.**

The Retirement Reboot

The COVID-19 pandemic has accelerated the trend of unorthodox retirements. While some still choose a firm retirement date, many are exploring flexible options: reducing hours, consulting, or starting new ventures. Ryan Reynolds, actor and entrepreneur, has said, "Retirement is reprioritizing your life." This idea leaves room for a personalized retirement plan that fits your life and passions. I like the phrase "**refirement**."

In refirement, a person fires/terminates themselves from an old way of doing things. They might keep the same job but approach it in an entirely different way. So you fire yourself from your old job and simultaneously regain a passion, or *fire*, for the new way of doing things. Whether it's a different approach to the same job, a different job but the same work, or an entirely new gig altogether, refirement is a complete reprioritization of how you'll engage the world through work until you don't want to work anymore.

The State of Retirement Savings

Establishing a retirement nest egg is essential regardless of your approach to retirement. The sad truth is that many Americans are woefully unprepared for retirement. Here are the median retirement savings by age group for 2022:[3]

Age	Median Amount Saved for Retirement
Less than 35	$18,880
35 to 44	$45,000
45 to 54	$115,000
55 to 64	$185,000
65 to 74	$200,000
75-plus	$130,000

To put this data into perspective, let's assume someone in the 65 to 74 age group invests their $200K portfolio with an expected return of around 5 percent. If we assume they start taking funds from this account at age 67 for the next 20 years and draw the account to zero, they can take just over $1,300 per month. Even when their savings are coupled with

---

[3] Federal Reserve Board. (2023). *Changes in U.S. family finances from 2019 to 2022: Evidence from the Survey of Consumer Finances*. Board of Governors of the Federal Reserve System. https://doi.org/10.17016/8799

Social Security, we know that individuals live on very little in the prime of their retirement. Also, it should be noted that of this age group, only 51 percent have a retirement account of any type. These figures from the Federal Reserve's 2022 Survey of Consumer Finances should worry everyone—governments, employers, and families alike.

Adding to the challenge is the fact that Social Security is not the safety net it once was. By 2035 the number of Americans over 65 will nearly double, but the system is expected to bring in only 83 cents for every dollar needed. In 2020 the average Social Security benefit was $1,446 per month, barely above the poverty line for a two-person household. Possible solutions range from raising the retirement age to increasing taxes or even overhauling the system completely.

How This Book Works for You

As the above points illustrate, the retirement landscape today is more complex than ever—but that means there are also more opportunities and choices than ever. I wrote this book to encourage everyone to save and invest for retirement. The goal is to make Social Security a nice bonus rather than a necessity. But with so many books, articles, and advisors out there, why another book? **Well, despite all the information and resources available, many people still feel overwhelmed and confused about how to save effectively for retirement.**

This book is for everyone—from those just starting their careers to those nearing retirement. Whether you're a recent graduate, midcareer, or late in the game, there are strategies here for you. I'll address common questions like when to start saving, how much to defer, which accounts to use, and which investments to choose.

Here are some of the specific insights and advantages you will gain from the book, depending on where you are in your retirement journey:

> **New-to-Career (Ages 22 to 35):** By reading this book, you will unlock the secrets of starting your financial journey on the right foot. You'll discover how powerful compounding can be when you start saving early and consistently—even with small amounts. The book simplifies complex financial concepts, making them easy to understand, so you can confidently navigate your 401(k) and make smart money moves. You'll learn practical steps to maximize your employer's matching contributions—essentially free money—and set yourself on a path to becoming a millionaire by retirement. Start now, and you'll thank yourself later!

> **Midcareer (Ages 35 to 50):** This book is your guide to navigating the financial pressures of midlife while keeping your retirement goals on track. You'll find strategies to manage competing priorities like mortgages and education costs without sacrificing your future. This book offers clear, actionable advice on boosting your 401(k) contributions, minimizing fees, and making wise investment choices that balance growth and stability. With practical tips tailored to

your stage in life, it empowers you to take control of your retirement savings and make meaningful progress, even if you feel like you're playing catch-up.

Preretirees and Late Bloomers (Ages 50-plus): Don't worry—it's never too late to make a positive impact on your retirement. This book is packed with insights tailored for you, offering strategies to maximize catch-up contributions, reassess your retirement timeline, and even explore the benefits of working a bit longer to enhance your nest egg. With real-life success stories of people who improved their financial futures later in life, it provides practical steps and encouragement to help you create a solid retirement plan. You'll gain the knowledge and confidence to take control of your financial future, ensuring that your retirement years are as comfortable and secure as possible.

What Makes This Book Unique

So, why should you read on? Amid the crowded field of books on retirement advice, I felt the need to add a more human, intuitive touch, focusing not just on data and theory but also on the *psychological* and *emotional* facets of preparing for retirement. I also wanted to offer advice that felt tailored to the present, taking into account, among other factors, the rise of nontraditional careers and experimental approaches to retirement, like the FIRE movement, as well as nontraditional assets such as cryptocurrency. In *Becoming a 401(k) Millionaire*, I simplify complex financial concepts and make them accessible, actionable, and relatable through real-life success stories that inspire and motivate.

Your Retirement Journey

Over two decades, my company, Human Investing, has guided thousands of individuals and families through the process of saving, investing, and retiring. This book distills those experiences into practical advice you can use to create your own successful retirement plan.

Thanks for picking up my book—I hope you enjoy it and find it helpful!

Sincerely,

Peter

PART I: MAPPING THE RETIREMENT TERRAIN AND SECURING YOUR FUTURE

CHAPTER 1

FROM SMALL BEGINNINGS TO BIG DREAMS: THE POWER OF A 401(K)

Several years ago, I was working in our office when our receptionist called out for any available member of the retirement advisory team. Looking around, I noticed everyone else was either with a client or on the phone. Rather than just taking a message, I decided to take the call. Little did I know that this decision would be one of the many reasons I was compelled to write this book.

Meet Lula

On the other end of the line was Lula, an employee from a company in Rochester, New York, whose 401(k) plan we manage. She wanted to learn more about her company's retirement plan and the enrollment process. Lula, like many of our callers, shared a bit about her life. She had a child when she was young and was now working hard to ensure her child's future. Lula was 22 years old, earning around $25,000 per year, and hoped to improve her quality of life over time.

As Lula shared her story, I entered her information into our retirement calculator: 22[1] years old, earning $25,000 annually, with an expected retirement age of 65. I assumed a 9 percent annual return on her investments, a 2.5 percent rate of inflation, and that her funds would last until she was 85. I also assumed a 5 percent return on her invested dollars during retirement. Lula's contribution would be 5 percent of her gross annual salary, with her employer contributing an additional 4 percent annually.

What I saw on the screen brought a smile to my face. If these assumptions held, Lula would be a 401(k) millionaire, with total savings of over $1.4 million. Her monthly income from investments, after adjusting for inflation, would be $3,296.92—nearly 60 percent more than her current monthly compensation. Any other income, such as Social Security, would be a welcome addition.

Lula's Future

After I explained the results to Lula over the phone, she was thrilled and ready to enroll in her employer's plan. She now works knowing that her and her daughter's futures are secure. She works knowing that in her 60s, she will have a choice of whether to continue her career, pivot to another,

---

[1] According to the Federal Reserve Boards Survey of Consumer Finances (2022), less than one-half of individuals below the age of 35 have a retirement account.

or retire gracefully—all of these possible because she took an interest in her company-sponsored 401(k) plan.

A Call to Action

Lula's call changed her future and renewed my passion for helping others in the retirement plan industry. However, many employees miss out on retirement savings due to bad information or a lack of knowledge. Although there is plenty of blame to pass around for employees not taking advantage of company-sponsored retirement plans, ultimately we, as employees, need to do our part as we are the ones who stand to benefit the most from knowing.

Simple Steps to Success

Lula's path to becoming a 401(k) millionaire isn't magic—it's a straightforward formula:

1. Save a small portion of your paycheck consistently.

2. Work for a company that offers matching or profit-sharing contributions.

3. Ensure total savings (employee and employer contributions) are in the neighborhood of 10 percent or more.

4. Invest your retirement savings in a low-cost, age-based target retirement index fund.

If you understand these four steps and are ready to take charge of your wealth-building journey, you can close this book and start now. But for those who need more convincing details (most of you, I'm assuming)—read on!

The Snowball Effect

One of the primary reasons this formula works is compounding, which we will explore throughout the book. Compounding is like rolling a small snowball in the snow—it gets bigger the more you roll it. Albert Einstein allegedly called compound interest "the most powerful force in the universe," and Benjamin Franklin described it this way: "Money makes money. And the money that money makes, makes money." Time, consistency, and low fees are the key to maximizing your nest egg.

Imagine starting with a small snowball at 25 and rolling it for 40 years. How big would it be at that point? This analogy excites many when they are thinking about long-term investing. Undeniably, seeing a retirement account grow over 30 or 40 years is impressive.

Why You Should Invest in a 401(k)

Even if retirement feels far away, or if you never plan on retiring, investing in a 401(k) offers benefits:

Tax Advantages: Contributions to a traditional 401(k) are made with pretax dollars, reducing your taxable income for the year. This means you pay less in taxes now and defer them until retirement, when you may be in a lower tax bracket.

Employer Matching: Many employers offer to match a portion of your contributions, effectively giving you free money toward your retirement savings. For example, if your employer matches 50 percent of your contributions up to 6 percent of your salary, contributing that 6 percent ensures you get the full match.

Automatic Savings: 401(k) contributions are typically deducted directly from your paycheck, making it a seamless and automatic way to save. This "set it and forget it" approach helps you consistently build your retirement nest egg without having to think about it.

Compound Growth: Your 401(k) funds grow tax-deferred, meaning you don't pay taxes on investment gains each year. Over time, this allows your investments to compound, potentially leading to significant growth in your retirement savings.

High Contribution Limits: 401(k) plans have higher contribution limits compared to other retirement accounts like IRAs. As of 2024, you can contribute up to $23,000 annually,[2] with an additional $7,500 catch-up contribution if you're over 50.[3]

---

2 IR-2023-203.

3 Internal Revenue Service. (2023). *COLA increases for dollar limitations on benefits and contributions.* https://www.irs.gov/newsroom/cola-increases-for-dollar-limitations-on-benefits-and-contributions

Investment Options: 401(k) plans typically offer a range of investment options, including stocks, bonds, mutual funds, and target-date funds. This allows you to diversify your portfolio according to your risk tolerance and retirement timeline.

Loan and Hardship Withdrawals: While it's generally best to avoid tapping into your 401(k) before retirement, many plans allow for loans or hardship withdrawals in case of emergencies. This flexibility can provide a financial safety net in times of need.

Understanding the Stock Market and Index Funds

Not every story is as simple or successful as Lula's. She had an entry-level wage, a single household income, and diapers to pay for. Yet despite these factors, she figured out a way to save and invest for her future while also meeting her needs at home.

Many excuses prevent employees from saving for retirement, but the harsh reality is these excuses will only keep you from reaching your goals. As appealing as relying on Social Security or hoping for an inheritance might be, neither represents a reliable retirement strategy. Even in cases of financial hardship, it's often more important to cut discretionary spending than to not participate in your company-sponsored 401(k) plan.

Employees are also uneasy about the stock market, fearing it is a gamble.[4] But investing in the stock market (Specifically the S&P 500) has a 70-plus-percent success rate, with an average gain of over 10 percent since 1956.[5] Contrary to popular belief, the stock market is not a casino. And if it were, we would get to be the house and have the odds stacked in our favor.

I have already advocated for index funds, both in this chapter and the introduction. Given their importance, I'll briefly describe them here but also spend time throughout the book helping you understand more about them and why they are the investment of choice for retirement savers.

An index fund can be a mutual fund or an exchange-traded fund (ETF) that tracks a specific market category. Investing in an index fund often means diversification, low expenses, and long-term performance.

Diversification: Diversification is just a fancy way of saying you are not putting all of your eggs into one basket. An S&P 500 index fund invests in the 500 largest publicly traded companies in the United States, providing broad market exposure across various sectors, including technology, health care, finance, and consumer goods. This diversification

---

4 Ramezani, C. A., & Ahern, J. J. (2023). How do financial market outcomes affect gambling? *Journal of Risk and Financial Management*, *16*(6), 294.

5 Maverick, J. B. (2024, January 3). *S&P 500 average return and historical performance*. Investopedia. https://www. https://www.investopedia.com/ask/answers/042415/what-average-annual-return-sp-500.asp

helps mitigate risk as the fund is not overly reliant on the performance of any single company or sector.

Low Expense Ratios: One of the appealing features of S&P 500 index funds is their low expense ratios. Because these funds passively track the index rather than actively managing the investments, they have lower operating costs, which can lead to higher net returns for investors over time.

Long-Term Performance: As previously mentioned, the S&P 500 has delivered strong long-term returns, averaging around 10 percent annually over the past several decades. This performance makes S&P 500 index funds a popular choice for long-term investors looking to build wealth steadily over time.

Although there are other types of stock market indices, I mention the S&P 500 because it is one of the world's most widely tracked stock market indices and the S&P 500 index fund (which tracks the index) is a staple in most 401(k) fund lineups.

The Takeaway

Having a job should be the gateway to saving for retirement. And so the good news is anyone can secure their financial future by following simple steps and understanding the power of compounding. If you're ready to take charge, keep reading for more insights and strategies on becoming a 401(k) millionaire.

Key Points from Chapter 1

1. **The Power of Compounding:** Compounding interest is a powerful force for building wealth. Starting early and consistently investing allow your money to grow exponentially over time.

2. **Maximize Employer Contributions:** Achieving financial success with a 401(k) involves saving a portion of your paycheck, benefiting from employer contributions, ensuring total contributions are at least 10 percent, and investing in low-cost, age-based target retirement index funds.

3. **Benefits Beyond Retirement:** Investing in a 401(k) offers immediate tax benefits, helps maintain a budget by encouraging saving, and grows wealth through employer matching—even if you plan to never retire.

4. **Start by Saving Early:** Lula's story illustrates how even with a modest income, consistent saving and investing can lead to becoming a 401(k) millionaire. Her journey emphasizes the importance of starting early and making informed decisions.

5. **Overcoming Market Fears:** Despite fears and misconceptions, investing in the stock market is not gambling. Historically, the stock market has offered

a 70 percent chance of making money each year, with an average gain of over 10 percent.

6. **Understanding Index Funds:** Index funds, including mutual funds and ETFs, provide broad market exposure and reduce risk by including hundreds or thousands of stocks. They are a straightforward way to invest without picking individual stocks.

7. **Take Control of Your Future:** Relying on Social Security or hoping for an inheritance is an unreliable retirement strategy. Saving and investing consistently are crucial, even during financial hardships.

CHAPTER 2

YOUR RETIREMENT ROAD TRIP: FROM POINT A TO 401(K)

In chapter 1, I shared some of the basics of a 401(k), such as the importance of saving early, the power of compounding, and investing in low-cost index investments. Nevertheless, at the top of the list is a company's willingness to match what you put into your plan. A company match is not just a sign that they want to partner with you in your retirement journey; it also indicates how the company prioritizes people.

I have three adult children, and the topic of retirement often comes up. I would give you the same advice I've given my children and the same advice we've dispensed at our firm for 20 years: **Make who you work for (if you are not self-employed) more than just about a paycheck.**

The Salary Trap: Why Pay Isn't Everything

When you're starting your career in your late teens or 20s, it's easy to be lured by the salary or hourly wage a company offers. But hold your horses! Before you sign on the dotted line, there's something crucial you need to consider: the company's 401(k) plan.

The salary trap is just as important a consideration for first-time job seekers as it is for those switching jobs. Don't jump ship for a higher salary—consider the quality of the new employer's 401(k) plan. A stellar 401(k) plan can be a game-changer for retirement savings.

Similarly, if you are already employed and are just now learning about 401(k) plans, determine whether your company's plan has a company match and other vital features, such as low-cost investment options. If the plan stacks up and is considered a quality 401(k) offering, lucky you! If not, you might consider switching to a company that offers a superb retirement plan and is willing to partner with you on your retirement journey.

What the Heck Is a 401(k), Anyway? The 401(k) Defined

A 401(k) is a retirement savings plan sponsored by an employer. The 401(k) name comes from the 401(k) subsection that was added to the Internal Revenue Code. The 401(k) plan is part of the 1978 Revenue Act passed by Congress to promote retirement savings. For those wanting to nerd out on this history, we will discuss more in chapter 4.

This type of retirement account helps workers save and invest a portion of their paychecks before taxes are taken out. Taxes are not paid until the money is withdrawn from the account (an exception is a Roth 401(k), but more on that later). Simply put, a 401(k) is a way for you to contribute pre-tax money into a savings account and select from a lineup of funds in which to invest those dollars so they will grow.

Getting Started: The Simplicity of a 401(k) Plan

One of the many remarkable benefits of a 401(k) plan is its simplicity. To get started, determine if your employer offers any retirement plan or 401(k) specifically. (As previously shared, working for an employer that offers a 401(k) plan is a must!) If so, ask for the enrollment package and call the institution in charge of your plan.

If you had one of the plans my company oversees, you would speak with one of our retirement education advisors. We would walk you through how to sign up, then discuss your investment options, how much to contribute from your paycheck, and how to select between the traditional 401(k) plan and the Roth option (if your plan offers it).

There is a lot to think about, but I intend to walk you through all of it in the pages ahead. **If your company, or one you are considering, does not have a retirement plan such as a 401(k), I would find a company that does.**

The 401(k) Factor: Why It Should Top Your List

So whether you are looking to start your first job, have been working for years, or have been with a company and are just now learning about the 401(k), a company's 401(k) plan isn't just a nice perk—it's a powerful tool for your future financial security. Meaningful qualities of top-rated 401(k) plans include:

1. *Company Match:* Look for companies that offer a solid match on your contributions. For example, if a company matches 50 percent of your contributions up to 6 percent of your salary, that's another 3 percent that goes into your retirement plan. That little extra is free money—consider it a bonus you don't have to work additional hours for.

2. *Profit Sharing:* Some companies go a step further by offering profit-sharing plans. This means they contribute a portion of their profits to your 401(k) account. The vesting schedule (how long you must stay with the company to claim these funds) is also crucial. The faster you're vested, the sooner you can fully own those contributions.

3. *Plan Management:* Investigate how well the 401(k) plan is managed. Low-cost investment options and a variety of funds to choose from can make a significant difference in how much your savings grow over time.

Red Flags: When to Think Twice

Take note if a company talks the talk but doesn't walk the walk when it comes to its 401(k) plan. A poorly managed 401(k) or a lack of employer contributions might signal that the company doesn't prioritize its employees' long-term well-being. Ask yourself, if they won't invest in your future, how well will they treat you now?

The Employer's Commitment to You

To be clear, a company with a robust 401(k) plan is demonstrating its commitment to its employees' future. This clearly indicates that they value their team and are willing to invest in their long-term success. In contrast, a company with a lackluster 401(k) plan or one that doesn't offer a 401(k) to begin with might not have your best interests at heart.

The data supports employees being suspicious about employers that don't offer 401(k)s or choose to offer a plan but fail to support it with low-cost fund options or matching contributions. There is a clear connection between 401(k) plan performance and corporate financial performance.[6]

Choosing the right company to work for involves looking beyond the immediate paycheck. By prioritizing employers with robust 401(k) plans, you're setting yourself up for a secure financial future. Remember, a company that invests in your retirement is a company that invests in you. So when weighing your options, think about your long-term goals and choose an employer that aligns with your vision for a prosperous future.

Do Your Homework: Plan Before You Enroll

If you are just now hearing about 401(k) plans and are already at a company that offers one, you'll want to learn

---

6 T. Rowe Price. (2018). *Where 401(k) design and corporate profitability cross paths.*

about what a 401(k) is and why it's crucial. But while you do not need to be a financial expert to enroll, you must ask yourself, **"How will I earn an income when I'm no longer working?"** The quest to answer that simple question should be enough to find a solution for your retirement objectives. If you already work for an employer with a 401(k), you are likely not far away from being able to answer that question well.

It is essential to note that nobody should care more about your retirement than you. Before enrolling, spend the time necessary to understand your company 401(k) plan. Doing so can pay huge long-term dividends for you and your family. Getting up to speed on the 401(k) plan options may significantly affect how soon you can retire and with what lifestyle.

Different Types of Employer-Sponsored Plans

For those of you thinking, "I don't have a 401(k) plan," please keep in mind a 401(k) is just one type of employer-sponsored retirement account. There are a host of other plan types, and we will discuss a few of them here.

A 401(k) is the most common retirement savings account, so I will use the term 401(k) throughout this book in place of 403(b) or any other form of corporate retirement account. The main distinction between a 401(k) and a 403(b) is that a 403(b) is a retirement savings plan available primarily to workers in public education, nonprofits, health care, and religious institutions. I will also address individual retirement accounts (IRA) and why, in some cases, it makes more sense to open your own IRA instead of investing in the company-sponsored 401(k) plan. More information about alternatives to 401(k) plans will be offered in the next chapter (chapter 3).

Roth 401(k): Tax Benefits Today, Savings Tomorrow

The Roth 401(k) became a consideration for employees in 2006. Roth is both a feature within a 401(k) account and a stand-alone retirement account that allows the saver to contribute after-tax dollars. Putting your dollars into the Roth bucket within your 401(k) account requires consideration. Here's the benefit: within a 401(k) account, both low- and high-wage earners can contribute to the Roth bucket. That may not be true if you have a stand-alone Roth IRA account. This means that Roth IRA accounts have eligibility gates, so if you earn too much money, you may not be eligible to contribute to a Roth IRA account. However, the compensation maximums don't apply to the Roth 401(k). So whether you earn $18 an hour or $180K a year, you are eligible for Roth 401(k). In my view, the greatest benefit to a participant who chooses the Roth bucket within her 401(k) is that the taxes have already been paid in this scenario, so when money is taken out at retirement, there are no taxes to be paid on the contributed amounts and all profits are distributed without having to pay taxes.

Another great reason to choose the Roth 401(k) option is that there is no requirement to begin taking the money at a certain age—if money has not been withdrawn up to that point. This is not true for dollars in the pretax bucket. If you have been a good saver for years, this bucket of money could become something you leave to your loved ones as an inheritance, or you could blow it on self-indulging luxury. Either way, it's your money; you saved it, and you choose what to do with it!

Matching: Free Money from Your Employer

Previously, I mentioned the importance of having a company match. I'll dive a little deeper into the "why" here. Advanced homework can pay off big-time if your plan has a match. Remember, I'm not talking about dating or coordinating your shirt with your tie; I'm talking about free money. "Matching" is an industry term that describes an employer's contribution to an employee's retirement account.

Here is how it works: When an employee contributes to their 401(k) account, the employer matches a portion of that contribution up to a limit. These contributions are often capped at a certain level, but many employers offer some match. A typical company match starts at 3 percent of an employee's wages and can go up to 4 percent if an employee contributes 5 percent of his own money. This might seem like funny math, so let's break it down: Companies that use this formula will match 100 percent of your contribution up to 3 percent of your wages. From there, the company match goes down to 50 percent of your contribution to the next 2 percent of your contribution, up to 5 percent of the total wages you're contributing.

If this causes you brain pain and brings back memories of a bad math class, you are not alone! To keep things from getting too confusing, let's talk in dollars.

- If your salary is $100 and you put in $3 (3 percent of your salary), based on the above matching formula, the company would also put in $3.

- If you bump up your contribution to $4 (4 percent of your salary), you get a company match of $3.50.

- If you bump your contribution up to $5 (5 percent of your salary), your company will match it with $4. These company dollars are "free money" to you.

Too often, we sit down with an employee whose company has a matching feature in its 401(k) plan but the employee fails to contribute enough to receive the full match. Suppose your company has a match but money is tight. In that case, you will want to contribute—at a minimum—up to the contribution percent at which there is no longer a company contribution for any dollars you put into the plan. In other words, **you should contribute as much as you need to get all the "free money" you can**. The difference between working with a company that has a match and one that does not can be significant when it comes to what you can save over your working lifetime.

Here is a quick comparison that highlights the importance of working for an employer that offers a match versus one that does not.

Scenario 1: With Company Match
- Initial annual savings: $60,000 * (6% + 3%) = $5,400
- Growth rate: 9%

- Total savings after 30 years: $1,070,376.88

Scenario 2: Without Company Match
- Initial annual savings: $60,000 * 6% = $3,600
- Growth rate: 9%
- Total savings after 30 years: $713,584.64

Difference in Total Retirement Savings
The individual with the company match accumulates $1,070,376.88 over thirty years, while the individual without the company match accumulates $713,584.64 over the same period.

Thus, after 30 years, the individual who benefits from the company match has an additional $356,792.24 in retirement savings. This substantial difference highlights the critical impact of employer contributions on long-term retirement savings.

Vesting: When Employer Contributions Become Yours

Be aware, however, that seeing the benefits of matching might require a certain tenure length. Vesting is a term typically associated with a type of company match in a 401(k) plan, and it means the dollars are not yours right away. These dollars are deposited into your 401(k) account but are subject to a vesting schedule, which is a period of time before a match becomes fully yours. A typical vesting schedule is five years, which means that with each year a percentage of these dollars becomes yours, until the fifth year, when the entire amount is yours.

If your plan has a company match, it will specify if these dollars are yours immediately or if you get them over time (i.e., they're vested) or if it's a combination. One reason companies use a vesting schedule is to help retain good people. Further, a typical company contribution that is often subject to a vesting schedule is profit sharing. When looking at your plan and the company match, be sure to learn which company match dollars are yours right away and which are yours after the vesting period. This information will be helpful to you if you leave the company.

Automatic Enrollment: The Easy Way In

Just because the benefits of a 401(k) plan are quite obvious—as outlined above—doesn't mean every employed American is taking advantage of them. According to the March 2022 report from the Bureau of Labor Statistics, just 66 percent of private-sector employees had access to a 401(k) plan and there was an overall participation rate of below 50 percent. In an effort by companies to get enrollment up to 100 percent of their eligible workforce, employers are increasingly adopting automatic enrollment; the popularity of this approach stems from employers' desire for employees to benefit from the program and the percentage of employees who do not participate. With the government allowing and encouraging auto enrollment, if it is not already a part of your plan, it may by soon. While I believe auto enrollment to be a helpful tool, there are a few things to be aware of so you are not caught off guard.

Beginning in 2025, almost every new 401(k) and 403(b) plan must have an eligible automatic contributions arrangement policy (EACA), including an automatic enrollment rate between 3 percent and 10 percent, and automatic increase of 1 percent per year up to a maximum of at least 10 percent.

If your employer has auto enrollment, you'll need to determine if there is a matching contribution (that "free money" we discussed). Just ask the person who would typically help you with a human resources–related question or call the company that oversees your plan; either one will be able to tell you if you have a match.

If you have a match and have been auto-enrolled, it's probably a good thing because your company has just saved you from going through the enrollment process alone. However, if you've been auto-enrolled and there is no match, that may not be in your best interests, and further scrutiny is required to determine if putting money into the plan is still the best choice for you.

The first thing to consider is the deferral percentage at which you've been auto-enrolled. That percentage typically isn't where you'll need it to be, but some employees assume it's "just fine" and never change it. This can be a big mistake. Determine the amount you need or want to defer and if necessary, go in and change the deferral amount to what makes sense for you and your retirement, rather than accepting some preselected amount that is not customized to you and the standard of living you want in retirement.

Many professional advisors recommend deferring at least 10 percent of your income into your retirement. Then, if you can, increase this to 15 percent as soon as possible. Increase this amount by 1 percent each year if you can.

The list below shows the suggested amount of money you should have saved in your 401(k) plan for different ages:

- 30 years old—1x your income

- 35 years old—2x your income

- 40 years old—3x your income

- 45 years old—4x your income

- 50 years old—6x your income

- 55 years old—7x your income

- 60 years old—8x your income

- 67 years old—10x your income

Keep in mind that these are the minimum suggested amounts. If you can put more, do it. Set up your 401(k) so that it aligns with your long-term goals.

The other major factor to consider when auto-enrolled is the investment the company has put in. This is super important, given that no two retirees are the same. If you, like me, plan to work well into your 70s, then the off-the-shelf investment your company preselected for you may be a poor choice. So do your homework: find out your auto-enrolled investment choice and, as with the deferral percentage, change your investment election if necessary.

If your company auto-enrolls employees but does not match their contributions, then you have some things to consider. The first consideration is whether you'll contribute more than $7,000 (if you are younger than 50) or $8,000 (if you are older than 50). These amounts are the maximum contribution to IRAs as of 2024. The two figures are key because if you don't plan to contribute more than these amounts to your 401(k) plan, you are most likely better off opening an IRA account and minimizing your overall costs. This approach is an alternative to being automatically enrolled in a plan without a matching contribution.

Although you cannot contribute as much to an IRA, it is a great, low-cost entry into retirement savings for many American workers, with similar tax benefits. Given there are administrative charges with 401(k) plans, in most cases, a 401(k) will be more expensive to manage than an IRA.

SECURE 2.0 Act: New Laws, New Benefits

Not often do we get beneficial laws passed by Congress, especially tax-advantaged laws. The SECURE (Setting Every Community Up for Retirement Early) 1.0 Act was passed in 2019 and increased retirement benefits for everyone in the United States. The law increases the amount we can put into our retirement accounts and how long we can wait to withdraw from them. It also increased access to 401(k) (or similar) accounts for people who did not have good enough access before.

SECURE 2.0 was passed at the very end of 2022 and updated the 1.0 version of the law with even better benefits. Here are the highlights:

- Retirement contribution limits to IRAs were increased from $6,000 in 2022 to $6,500 in 2023.

- The catch-up contributions for workers 50 and older are now $7,500, up from $6,500 in 2022.

- The age limit increases to 73 from 72 for required minimum distributions (RMDs) in traditional accounts. This means that we do not have to touch our 401(k) money until we are 73. As the law stands, this will increase again to age 75 by 2033.

- Starting in 2025, individuals 60 to 63 can increase their catch-up contributions to $10,000 annually!

- Individuals who did not take out RMD at the required age used to be subject to a 50 percent excise tax. This has been lowered to 25 percent.

- Roth 401(k) accounts will not be subject to RMD while the owner is alive.

There are other changes that come with the new SECURE 2.0 law, and we will discuss them in different sections of this book as they relate to a broad field of financial topics. What is essential is that contribution limits have increased. Another thing to note is that tax laws change frequently, usually with each new Congress, which happens every two years, but the laws can change as often as every year. Individuals must keep up with tax laws to understand how this may change their retirement benefits. This is why it is highly advisable to hire a tax attorney, financial planner, or CPA.

Doing Your Homework: Real-Life Examples

Doing your homework and gaining some knowledge about your plan can pay off in real money. I will show you how significant the impact can be with the example below. Let's look at two employees and see how personal responsibility affected their decisions and experience with their company's 401(k) plan.

First up is Don. At the recommendation of this book, Don spent some time understanding the details of his 401(k) plan. Don noticed that the plan auto-enrolled all participants and that there was no company match. He read further and discovered that his plan's fees averaged 2.05 percent. Given the high fees, no matching contribution, and that he would not be contributing more than $5,000 per year, he opted to open an IRA account instead.

On the other hand, we have Rick. Rick, not having read our book or the enrollment packet, did not notice that he was automatically enrolled. He, too, was going to contribute less than $5,000 per year. When after a year he noticed he had been paying into a retirement account, he decided to leave it alone. Note that he was paying more than 2 percent to buy a fund similar to Don's.

For the calculation, I have both Rick and Don earning $36,000 per year, with 2.5 percent wage inflation. Don earns 9.05 percent on his investment, and Rick earns 7 percent instead of 9.05 percent because of a 2.05 percent fee reduction. We assume they are both 22 and will work for another 40 years. The great news is that they both saved! The bad news is that with just a little more time and effort spent researching his company's 401(k) plan, Rick could have opted out (like Don) and potentially earned $691,650 more, or $1,700 a month more during retirement—all for doing a little reading. While an extreme example, this is a situation that plagues retirement plan participants and is the cause of billions of dollars of avoidable losses due to fees each year.

The other place auto enrollment can sting is in the fund in which the dollars are enrolled. Unfortunately, too many retirement plan providers direct automatically enrolled participants to their own mutual funds as the default. This isn't great for the employee, especially when lower-cost and potentially better-performing investments exist.

Recently, I was reviewing a 401(k) plan in which participants were automatically enrolled in the plan's proprietary mutual fund, where the costs were three times those of a similar low-cost index mutual fund. Retirement plan participants cannot assume the 401(k) service provider has their best interests in mind. Spending a little time to get up to speed on the investment options and costs, and the features of your retirement plan, will pay huge dividends over time.

Even if automatic enrollment is a good thing for you and your coworkers, the fund you are placed in may not be the best choice. If you have been automatically enrolled in your plan or you are in a fund run by the same company offering your retirement plan, it is your responsibility to make sure you are invested the way you want to be. If you are not and want to make a change, with a little learning, you can find a better option that will give you the best chance to retire with the maximum number of financial resources. Always remember that you are your own best advocate!

401(k) Taxes, Penalties, and Restrictions

Part of advocating for yourself is understanding the full extent of the 401(k) landscape. The 401(k) investment vehicle is one of the best retirement options available to most people. However, it does not come without some drawbacks. There are certain situations where 401(k) accounts may not be good for you, and you need to be aware of these.

The first drawback is that you are restricted as to what you can invest in. You only get to choose investment options in your company's plan. Another downside is that 401(k) plans are typically more expensive than IRAs, which we will describe in more detail in the next few chapters. The managing company may charge high managing fees or administrative fees. The industry average is a little over 1 percent, but some charge closer to 2 percent. You want to find fees lower than the average, less than 1 percent.

The process of rolling over the 401(k) when you leave the company is doable, but it can take a long time and can be cumbersome. The tax implications can be complicated and can change yearly:

- The IRS early withdrawal penalty is a 10 percent tax on any money taken out before the age of 59 1/2.

- Additionally, you must pay income tax on the withdrawn amount according to your current tax bracket and the current year. The total tax penalty for taking money early can be astronomical.

- Early withdrawals can wipe away any tax savings and growth your account experienced, not to mention the emotional loss of losing value over the money that you sacrificed to save and invest. You are also missing the possible gains and opportunity cost your money could be earning.

If you absolutely must take money out, consider a loan (see the next section) because you will not be penalized the 10 percent in this scenario. You can also look at the "hardship clause" to withdraw without penalty. For example, in 2020, the IRS and Congress allowed people to take money out of their retirement, penalty free, to help families that were struggling during COVID-19.

The IRS has a table of hardship exceptions that can avoid penalties. You can find that on the irs.gov website under "Retirement Topics: Tax on Early Distributions." From this site, examples include armed service members being called to active duty, paying medical bills and health insurance, the individual having become disabled, someone owing money to the IRS, one's housing situation being critical, etc.

We want to make sure we get this point across: pulling from a 401(k) account, penalty free or not, is the last-resort scenario and we advise against this at all costs.

Loans: When Borrowing from Your 401(k) Is Necessary

Taking a loan from your 401(k) account is not preferable, but it is sometimes necessary. Life can throw us a few curveballs, and we are not always prepared. If at some point you need a loan, make sure you understand how it works and what your costs will be.

With most providers, when you borrow from your 401(k) account, you will pay a setup fee. I have seen loan setup fees ranging from $75 to $125. Beyond the setup fee, you will also pay interest on the loan balance. The amount you can take out against your 401(k) account is capped at $50,000 or 50 percent of your account balance, whichever is less. These are the up-front costs you will agree to when taking a loan against your own 401(k) account, but there is an additional cost that participants do not always consider.

One of the biggest downsides to taking a loan from your account is the consequences you face if you lose your job or leave the company before the loan is paid off. Generally speaking, once you leave a company with a balance remaining on your loan, you must pay the balance off in full. But what if you can't pay off the loan at that time? When a loan is not paid off upon leaving the company, the balance is considered a distribution from the plan, and you must pay both taxes and penalties. I have seen this happen to too many individuals to count, and in the end, it costs them dearly. Learning about 401(k) loans and the potential taxes and penalties might help you avoid a painful experience or unwanted liabilities.

Opt-Out Scenarios: When Life Throws a Curveball

Emergencies happen, and sometimes we have no control over certain events. This is why it is crucial to have a healthy emergency fund set up outside of your retirement. Still, something may happen that will require funds from your emergency fund, your income, other liquid assets, and your 401(k).

Before you pull from your 401(k), see if you can solve the cash flow problem by stopping your contributions to the account. This is called opt-out service, and it is simple and free. You can always start contributing later. You may be going through a tough season of life and dealing with losing your house or an unprecedented medical expense. Stopping your contributions will free up cash to help you manage the crisis.

If you are struggling with consumer debt (credit cards, auto loans, student loans, etc.) and unable to pay those loans off in a reasonable time, it is advisable that you stop retirement contributions. In some cases (particularly when we see credit card debt), the rate your bank is charging you for the loan is far greater than a person can earn in a diversified investment portfolio. If this is your situation, consider pausing your retirement account contributions and redirecting those funds to the debt. Soon enough the debt will be paid for, and once again you can start contributing to your retirement account.

Automatic Increase: Let Your Savings Grow

Before we move on to summing up the chapter, let's discuss automatic increase. This feature is often attached to a plan with automatic enrollment. As the name implies, this feature automatically increases the amount of money you place in your retirement account by 1 or 2 percent each year, up to a certain limit. The company determines the annual increase and the limit at which the auto increase will stop. My company has this feature on our plan, capped at 10 percent. If someone enters the plan contributing 5 percent, her percentage will increase yearly until it reaches 10 percent. The auto increase is meant to help change participant behavior in a way that will benefit employees down the road. The increased savings can be timed with salary increases so that individuals begin contributing more to their retirement accounts while their take-home pay increases.

The one thing you need to look out for with this feature is your personal budget. If your monthly cash flow (i.e., money coming in and going out) is tight, having an extra $30 go to your retirement account may not be possible. I have seen many employees working hard to pay their bills for whom having even $30 or $50 more go into their retirement accounts versus their bank accounts might be the difference between making rent or not. If auto increase is a hardship for you, find out if your plan has it and if you can opt out. That said, this is a great feature in the vast majority of cases.

Navigating the Road to Retirement Success

Embarking on the journey to a secure retirement can seem daunting, but it becomes an exciting adventure with the right tools and knowledge. Understanding your 401(k) plan, knowing the options available, and making informed decisions are critical steps to ensuring your financial future. Remember, it's not just about the destination but the journey itself. Stay proactive, keep learning, and make the most of every opportunity to secure the retirement you deserve. You've got this—your road to retirement success starts now!

Key Points from Chapter 2

1. **Understanding 401(k) Basics:** A 401(k) is a retirement savings plan sponsored by an employer, allowing employees to save and invest a portion of their paycheck before taxes. Knowing the basics of your 401(k) plan, including contribution limits and investment options, is essential for effective retirement planning.

2. **The Importance of Employer Matching:** Employer matching is "free money" that can significantly boost your retirement savings. Always contribute enough to get the full match offered by your employer to maximize this benefit.

3. **Roth 401(k) Option:** The Roth 401(k) allows after-tax contributions, and withdrawals during retirement

are tax-free. This option is available to all income levels and offers flexibility and tax advantages in retirement.

4. **Vesting Schedules:** Understand your plan's vesting schedule, which dictates when employer contributions become fully yours. Vesting schedules are designed to retain employees, and knowing them helps you make informed decisions about your retirement savings.

5. **Automatic Enrollment and Increase:** Many employers use automatic enrollment to increase participation in retirement plans. Additionally, automatic increase features help employees gradually save more over time, often aligning with salary increases.

6. **Investment Choices and Costs:** Choose low-cost index funds to minimize fees and maximize returns. Be aware of the investment options available in your 401(k) plan and regularly review and adjust your investment strategy as needed.

7. **Tax Implications and Withdrawal Penalties:** Be aware of the tax implications and penalties for early withdrawals from your 401(k). Consider alternatives such as loans or hardship withdrawals only as a last resort, and always strive to keep an emergency fund outside of your retirement accounts.

CHAPTER 3

NAVIGATING YOUR PATH TO A MILLION-DOLLAR RETIREMENT

I hope you've already begun to see that investing in a 401(k) is like stepping into a unique investment wonderland. It's different from your usual stock market roller coaster for a few fabulous reasons. First, you've got a limited menu of options—think of it like a fancy restaurant with a curated list of top-notch dishes. Second, many corporate plans come with a bonus: your employer chips in some cash, like a fairy godmother. And finally, you're not required to touch your funds until you're 73, and with Roth 401(k) plans, you might never have to withdraw! These perks are golden when picking out funds to turbocharge your retirement savings.

It's not all smooth sailing all the time, however. When putting together your 401(k) investment options, your company might have hired an advisor to pick what they felt were the best options. Sometime they nail it, and other times, not so much. A stellar lineup should have easy-to-find names or ticker symbols so you can do a quick online search and get all the juicy details beyond what's on the 401(k) website. If the symbols of each fund are not readily available, you likely have a "group annuity" or insurance 401(k) offering. In that case, it will be more challenging to determine what funds you have and the costs associated with the investment.

If you have a group annuity, dig deep into the information your company gave you when you signed up for the 401(k) plan. In it, you'll be able to unearth the costs and performance of the investments—but be ready: the costs will be high, and the investment performance will typically be less due to the fees associated with this type of offering.

Now that you have a grasp on the logic and key benefits of the 401(k), in this chapter I want to discuss in greater depth some of the signposts you'll encounter along your path to becoming a 401(k) millionaire. Keep these topics in mind and you'll feel empowered and confident during the journey.

Understanding and Managing Fees

Now, about those costs—according to a Government Accountability Office (GAO) article focused on costs and 401(k) participation,[7] 40 percent of individuals participating in 401(k) plans answered fewer than half of the fee-related

---

[7] U.S. Government Accountability Office. (2021). *401(k) retirement plans: Many participants do not understand fee information, but DOL could take additional steps to help them* (GAO-21-357). https://www.gao.gov/products/GAO-21-357

questions correctly. Other essential highlights from the non-partisan GAO report include:

- **45% of participants** are not able to determine the cost of their investment fee from the information provided in disclosures

- **41% of participants** incorrectly believe that they do not pay any 401(k) plan fees

- **64% of participants** either believe they are not paying any fees or do not know if they are paying fees

- **81% of participants** do not know approximately how much they pay in fees or incorrectly believe they do not pay any fees at all

- **58% of participants** believe they are not knowledgeable about the impact of fees on their total retirement savings

- Only **7% of women** feel knowledgeable about the impact of fees, compared to **23% of men**

- **57% of participants** cannot identify the expense ratio for their investments when labeled differently in disclosures

- **63% of participants** do not understand that asset-based investment fees reduce their returns

These are shocking statistics, though not surprising given the conversations I have with 401(k) participants—readers of this book should refuse to be a statistic because you know better.

The Department of Labor (DOL) is the federal agency that enforces labor laws in the United States. When it comes to your 401(k) or other company-sponsored retirement plans, think of the DOL as your investment watchdog, sniffing out high fees to ensure more of your hard-earned cash stays with you, not lining the pockets of some big mutual fund company. Fees can vary depending on factors like cash flow, the number of participants, and average balances. While you'll always have to pay something, aim for fees under 1 percent.

Plans with fewer employees may be at the 1 percent level, while plans with hundreds or even thousands of employees may have fees well below 0.5 percent. Regardless, a slightly higher fee might be worth it if it comes with extras like tax planning or investment advice. But if your basic 401(k) charges a few percent or more, it's time to grab your savings and head for the hills!

Even with the DOL in your corner, costs vary from plan to plan. In my view, there are three different reasons expenses are higher in some plans and lower in others: fees can vary because of the type of professional hired to guide the plan, their approach to fund selection (active or passive), and whether the plan is large or small.

Advisors, Fiduciaries, and Your Wallet

All right, let's talk about advisors and why they matter regarding your 401(k) plan costs. Think of fiduciary advisors as your financial superheroes. They're legally required to act in your best interest. This means they're like your money's best friend, always looking out for you and making sure you get the best deals on your investments.

Now, let's compare them to nonfiduciary brokers. These guys don't have the same legal obligations. They might recommend more profitable investments for themselves, not necessarily for you. Picture them as the salespeople at a car dealership who push you to buy the most expensive car on the lot because they get a bigger commission. When it comes to 401(k) plans, this can mean higher costs for you because they might pick investments with higher fees to boost their earnings.

Fund Selection: The Battle Between Passive and Active

Next up, fund selection. It sounds boring, but stick with me—it's essential and can save you a lot of money. Advisors have two main strategies: passive and active investing.

- *Passive Investing:* Think of passive investing like a chill surfer riding the market waves. These funds, like index funds, aim to match the market, not beat it. They're super low maintenance and have low fees because there's not much buying and selling going on. The result? More of your money stays in your account, growing over time.

- *Active Investing:* On the flip side, active investing is like a high-stakes chess game. Fund managers are constantly making moves, trying to outsmart the market. This means more research, more trading, and—you guessed it—higher fees. These costs can eat into your returns, making it harder for your money to grow.

Science and academia generally favor passive investing for most people. Studies show that passive funds often outperform active funds. So if you want to be a 401(k) millionaire, sticking with passive funds might be your best bet (see the SPIVA chart from chapter 5).

Size Matters: The Economy of Scale

Finally, let's talk about the size of your 401(k) plan. Size does matter, but in a good way! Larger plans (those with 100 or more employees) benefit from something called economies of scale. This is just a fancy way of saying that the more people and money in the plan, the cheaper it is per person. Big plans can negotiate lower fees because they bring in more business for the service providers. It's like getting a bulk discount at your favorite warehouse store.

On the other hand, smaller plans with fewer participants and less money tend to have higher costs. They don't have as much negotiating power, so they end up paying more per person. It's like buying single rolls of toilet paper instead of a jumbo pack—you're going to pay more per roll.

All of this matters because not all plans are built the same. And, despite the DOL standing in your corner to police bad-acting companies and advisors, you still need to identify a good plan from a bad one and high fees from lower ones. You will pay fees, so knowing what they are and whether your plan is a good value is essential. If you determine your plan is not a good value and could be better, consider asking your company about alternatives or if they'd be willing to add you to the 401(k) committee. The more you study your 401(k) plan, the better your chances of minimizing those pesky fees and maximizing your retirement savings.

Investment Fund Lineup: Less Is More

One practice you can use to check if your 401(k) plan is lacking is to dive deep into the fund menu. I look for a few things to determine if my options are reasonable: First, I look at the number of funds. Second, I look to see if there is a good mix of low-cost options from well-known fund companies. Finally, I make certain there is a nice suite of target-date mutual funds.

At the same time, when it comes to 401(k) investment lineups, less is definitely more. You might think having a plethora of options is a good thing, but in reality, too many choices can lead to decision paralysis and poor investment decisions.

When reviewing 401(k) fund lineups for clients, I typically see as few as 20 options, but sometimes plan participants can have 30 or more choices. Ideally, I would like to see 10 to 15 funds in a lineup. This range allows participants to avoid being overwhelmed by the number of choices while still ensuring that committees and advisors can feel confident they've done their job in diversifying the fund menu and providing ample choice for participants.

Think of it this way: a streamlined lineup helps you focus on making strategic choices rather than getting bogged down by too many options. Imagine walking into an ice cream shop with 100 flavors—it sounds great until you spend an hour deciding what to get and end up with something you're not even sure you like. A well-curated selection, like 10 to 15 solid flavors, makes choosing and enjoying your investment journey so much easier.

Diversified Low-Cost Options: The Building Blocks of Success

Diversification and low costs are the twin pillars of smart investing. A strong 401(k) line-up should feature a mix of low-cost funds across key investment categories.

Essential Categories to Include:

- *Large Cap:* These funds invest in big, established companies that offer steady growth. They are like the giant redwoods in your investment forest.

- *Mid Cap:* These funds target midsize companies that combine growth and stability, much like the versatile maple trees that balance the ecosystem.

- *Small Cap:* These funds invest in smaller companies with high growth potential, akin to young saplings that grow quickly but require more care.

- *International Developed:* These funds provide exposure to established economies outside the United States, adding global diversity to your portfolio.

- *International Emerging Markets:* Investing in emerging markets is like planting fast-growing bamboo—high risk but potentially high reward.

- *Bond Funds:* A range of low-cost bond funds provides stability and income, acting as the solid underbrush that supports and protects your investment forest.

The Magic of Target Date Funds

Target date funds are the simple, hassle-free way to invest your 401(k) savings. They automatically adjust your asset mix based on your expected retirement date, making them a convenient choice.

How They Function:

- *Set It and Forget It:* Choose a fund that matches your retirement year (e.g., 2040, 2050). The fund manager will take care of the rest, adjusting the asset allocation as time progresses.

- *Glide Path:* As you near retirement, the fund gradually shifts from riskier investments like stocks to more conservative ones like bonds. It's like your investments mellow out as you get closer to retirement.

- *Example:* If you plan to retire around 2050, you'd select a Target Date 2050 fund. Early on, the fund might be heavily invested in stocks for growth. As you age, it shifts more toward bonds to reduce risk, ensuring your nest egg is safer as retirement approaches.

Target date funds are perfect for those who prefer a hands-off approach, offering a diversified portfolio that evolves with your life stage. Plus, they usually come with low expense ratios, making them a cost-effective option.

For the most part, whether your plan offers 40 funds or 15, the investments you need will be in the lineup; you'll have to find them. It's rare today to see a fund menu lacking low-cost index mutual funds, which is to your benefit. Depending on the plan, finding the right funds with the lowest cost may take some work—but it's worth it.

The Importance of Knowing about the S&P 500

An index fund gives you broad exposure to a specific market, which is a smart way to invest for the long term. Take the S&P 500, whose benefits we've already begun to explore. This index fund includes 500 of the largest companies in the United States, offering a slice of the entire economy. It's a low-cost, low-hassle way to invest, with minimal buying and selling of stocks.

Why are index funds better than trying to pick individual stocks? For starters, investing in index funds means you're buying into the bulk of the US economy. Trying to pick the next Google or Amazon is incredibly tough, even for seasoned investors. Index funds spread your risk and simplify your life. Historically, they are less volatile and deliver higher average returns compared to picking individual stocks.

If I were to build the simplest investment portfolio, I'd go with a total stock market index fund focusing on the US economy. Personally, I use the Vanguard Total Stock Market Index Fund for my IRAs. My wife and I contribute to these funds annually, and we have no plans to change that approach.

A Real-Life Example

Consider an investor who started 25 years ago, putting $500 a month into the S&P 500 index fund. From January 1992 to December 2016 (I use this date range as it includes a good mix of good and bad market conditions), their total contribution of $150,000 would have grown to $472,464. That's an average annual return of 8.25 percent, with a total profit of $322,464. Consistent contributions over time can lead to significant wealth.

The beauty of index funds in a 401(k) is that they allow you to own pieces of major companies like Apple, Google, Facebook, Amazon, John Deere, General Electric, and Delta Airlines—all without breaking the bank.

If the same investor had contributed $400 a month (a total of $120,000), they'd end up with around $377,000, profiting by $257,000. Investing $300 a month in the S&P

500 over your career could result in impressive amounts of money:

Years	Year-End Total (Average Annual Return of 9%)
25	$305,000
30	$491,000
35	$776,000
40	$1.2 million

Is This Approach Right for You?

As you can no doubt see, the ease and simplicity of index funds are hard to beat. However, this type of investment is best for those who can handle market ups and downs without panicking. If you're someone who can stay invested even when the headlines scream doom, this might be the perfect strategy for you. On the other hand, if you'd lose sleep over a temporary 20 percent drop in your retirement account, you might want to explore other options. In a later chapter, we'll delve into behavioral economics to help you understand your risk tolerance better.

The power of consistent contributions and the stability offered by index funds can set you on a path to financial success. By sticking to a simple, disciplined investment strategy, you too can reap the benefits of the market's long-term growth. Remember, the key is to stay the course and avoid letting short-term fluctuations derail your plans. Whether you're just starting or have been investing for years, the journey to becoming a 401(k) millionaire is well within reach with patience and perseverance.

More on Target Retirement Funds: Diversify like a Pro

Looking for more diversification that spans both US and international markets? Target retirement funds are your go-to solution, and they've become pretty mainstream. You can spot them easily by their names, which include a target date in five-year increments. The Vanguard Target Retirement 2025 Fund, to choose one, is a classic pick.

Here's the deal: Each target date corresponds to the year you plan to retire, assuming you'll be around 65. When you hit 65, the Vanguard fund typically has around 50 percent stocks (both US and non-US), with the rest in bonds or cash. By the time you're age 70, that mix shifts to about 35 percent stocks and more bonds, giving you a lower-risk portfolio.

If you're young with plenty of time ahead for investing, go for a fund with the furthest target date from today, like 2060. On the other hand, if you're starting later (say at age 40) or if you're a worrier who loses sleep over market dips, a closer date like 2040 might be a better fit.

Target date funds offer peace of mind. You don't have to check or rebalance your investments constantly. If you'd rather not worry about managing your portfolio, they are perfect for you. But if you're the DIY type who enjoys hands-on investing, you might prefer a different approach.

Tips, Common Mistakes, and Knowing Yourself

When it comes to investing, just like in life, mistakes happen. Three big ones to watch out for are picking the wrong mutual funds, mixing up too many target retirement funds, and not setting up automatic rebalancing. But don't worry—avoiding these pitfalls is easier than you think.

Unless you're a self-proclaimed investment wizard, stick around. For the rest of us (which is most of us), selecting a fund is as simple as picking an age-appropriate target retirement fund—just one! These funds are professionally managed, low-cost, and globally diversified. They automatically rebalance, becoming safer as you get closer to retirement. For example, owning the Vanguard Target Retirement 2035 fund means you're invested in four low-cost mutual funds covering thousands of companies. No need to juggle multiple funds or worry about rebalancing; it's all taken care of for you.

One Fund to Rule Them All
You only need one target-date fund because it offers all the variety you need. Owning multiple target-date funds is like ordering every dish on the menu when one entrée would have been perfect. Keep it simple and stick to one fund.

For the Growth-Hungry Investor
If you crave growth and can handle a bit more risk, consider a US total stock market index mutual fund inside your 401(k). This option isn't as academically sound and comes with more ups and downs, but it's straightforward. Despite the name, many of the companies in these funds earn a

significant portion of their revenue from outside the United States, giving you some international exposure without the added geopolitical and currency risks.

Balancing Risk and Reward
The more growth you seek, the more risk you'll need to take. If you opt for more than one fund and want to mimic the strategy of a target-date fund, set your account to rebalance automatically. This reduces risk over time and keeps your investments aligned with your goals.

Know Your Limits
Whatever your investment approach, know your limits— in terms of both time and emotional resilience. Investing should be a path to financial security, not a source of sleepless nights. Keep it simple, stay consistent, and you'll be well on your way to becoming a 401(k) millionaire.

Keep Emotions out of Investing
Mixing emotions with investing is like mixing oil and water— it just doesn't work. If I could write a one-chapter book, it would be all about keeping emotions out of your investment decisions. If you're someone who tends to react emotionally, acknowledge this and avoid making investment choices based on feelings alone.

An overly volatile (risky) portfolio can set you up for failure. It's better to invest conservatively and stick with it than to start aggressively and panic-sell when the market dips. In fact, investing when the market is down often feels counterintuitive but can be a smart move. We'll dive deeper into emotional investing in a later chapter.

Risk and Return: What You Need to Know
Over time, taking more risk in your investments generally leads to higher returns. But that doesn't mean you should be aggressive just for the sake of it. The best place to take risks is inside your retirement account, where you contribute small amounts regularly over your investing lifetime.

As you get closer to retirement, you'll need to dial back the aggression. This is a great conversation to have with a financial planner, as the right time to be less aggressive depends on how much you've saved and invested outside your 401(k).

The "Conservative" versus "Aggressive" Dilemma

Investors often label themselves "conservative" or "aggressive," but that characterization really depends on the asset and the account. For example, I consider myself conservative when it comes to one's home. Ideally, I'd like to see homeowners pay off their mortgages before retirement and have several years' worth of cash or safe, liquid investments on hand.

However, when it comes to your work-related retirement accounts, I recommend investing as aggressively as you can. The odds of this paying off are high.

To see how these contrasting approaches play out in the real world, let's compare two investors. One invests $500 a month in his 401(k), splitting it between the S&P 500 and a bond index fund. After 20 years, this conservative investor would have around $75,000 less than his coworker who invests only in the S&P 500. Over a lifetime, the difference could be about $1.3 million less.

Being aggressive over time can significantly boost your retirement savings, as long as you're strategic about it and manage your emotions. Also, don't forget to take advantage of alternative retirement accounts outside of your 401(k), as discussed in earlier chapters.

Investing should be a balance of strategy and emotional control. By understanding your risk tolerance and making informed decisions, you'll be well on your way to becoming a 401(k) millionaire.

In Conclusion

In the grand adventure of 401(k) investing, the journey is as crucial as the destination. By understanding your options, keeping an eye on fees, and choosing the right funds, you're setting yourself up for a prosperous future. Remember, the key to success is consistency, discipline, and a touch of patience. Avoid the pitfalls of emotional decision-making, and stay focused on your long-term goals. Whether you're just starting out or well on your way, the road to becoming a 401(k) millionaire is paved with smart choices and steady contributions. So buckle up, enjoy the ride, and watch your retirement dreams come to life!

Key Points from Chapter 3

1. **Limited Options, Big Benefits:** Investing in a 401(k) is like dining at a fancy restaurant with a curated menu. The limited investment options simplify decision-making, and many plans offer employer contributions, giving your savings an extra boost. Plus, with Roth 401(k) plans, you might never need to withdraw your funds!

2. **Understanding Your Fees:** Many investors don't fully grasp their 401(k) fees. The Department of Labor (DOL) ensures fees are reasonable, but it's essential to know what you're paying. Aim for fees under 1 percent and be wary of higher fees unless they come with valuable services.

3. **Advisors and Fiduciaries:** Fiduciary advisors are legally bound to act in your best interest, unlike non-fiduciary brokers who might push higher-fee investments. Choose a fiduciary advisor to keep your costs low and your investments sound.

4. **Passive vs. Active Investing:** Passive investing, like riding the market waves, is generally more cost-effective and often outperforms active investing, which involves frequent trading and higher fees. Stick with passive funds for steady growth.

5. **Size Matters:** Larger 401(k) plans benefit from economies of scale, leading to lower fees per participant. Smaller plans tend to have higher costs. If your plan's fees are high, consider discussing alternatives with your employer.

6. **Target Date Funds:** These funds automatically adjust your asset mix based on your retirement date, offering a hassle-free, diversified investment strategy. They're perfect for those who prefer a hands-off approach to investing.

7. **Keeping Emotions in Check:** Emotional investing can lead to poor decisions. Stick to a consistent, disciplined strategy and avoid panic-selling during market downturns. Recognize your risk tolerance and invest accordingly to stay on track toward becoming a 401(k) millionaire.

CHAPTER 4

THE POWER OF STARTING EARLY: BUDGETING AND SAVING FOR RETIREMENT

Now that you have a grasp on what to look out for once you begin your retirement planning journey, the next question is, inevitably, "*When* do I start?" This is one of the most essential questions that can be asked, and your response can change the trajectory of your entire retirement. If your answer to this question is *now*, it can mean retiring with more than you ever expected. Answering *now* can also allow you to consider retiring earlier than you planned—but you'll need to make some choices.

Saving for retirement might sound like something only "future you" needs to worry about, but trust me, it's a game-changer to start early. Step one: nail down a budget. Determine how much you can stash away each month without surviving on ramen noodles. Actually, now that I know the implications of saving early, I'd recommend ramen noodles every time if it meant I could contribute to a 401(k) now, particularly if your company matches your contributions. The earlier you start saving, the more you will have later—it's like giving your future self a giant high-five.

Even if you consider yourself financially responsible, getting started on budgeting or saving might seem daunting. This chapter is meant to make it all seem manageable. Trust me, it's worth it.

Budget Basics: Getting Started

All right, let's talk budgeting! Now, I know this book isn't all about budgeting, but it's such a big deal in your investing journey that we need to break down some basics. First, grab a pen, your phone, or whatever you use to jot stuff down, and list all your monthly expenses. Peek at your bank statements from the last couple of months to get the full scoop. Sort these expenses into categories like food, transportation, utilities, rent/mortgage, subscriptions, eating out, and insurance. Now you can see where all your money's going (spoiler: it's probably more on coffee than you'd like to admit).

Next up, figure out your household income. If you're flying solo, that's just your take-home pay after taxes and deductions (a.k.a. the money you actually get to keep). Add in any other sources of income like rental earnings or that generous birthday check from Grandma. Now you've got your income and expenses lined up for at least a month.

Now, the fun part: budgeting! Look for areas where you can cut back—like maybe skip a few takeout nights—to save more in your 401(k). If you've already trimmed all the fat, think about boosting your income or ramping up your savings. Budgeting isn't about living like a monk; it's about giving your money a purpose and hitting your goals with intention.

Choose Your Method: Old School, Spreadsheets, or Apps
There are plenty of ways to start a budget. Some folks love the old-school method: writing everything out on paper and adjusting manually. It's a bit tedious but super satisfying. Others prefer using an online spreadsheet—tons of free templates are out there. The modern (and arguably easiest) way? Budgeting apps on your phone. A quick search will show you the top free or paid apps, most with free trials. Pick what works best for you, and start giving your money some direction!

Visualize Your Budget: Sample Budget Example
For us visual learners, I have provided a sample budget below to help visualize the process. This budget is just a snapshot of a single young person's financial situation for one month.

Category	Amount
Groceries	$300
Going out	$300
Car/Gas/Transport	$200
Utilities	$150
Internet/Cell Data	$178

DR. PETER FISHER

Category	Amount
Rent	$1,200
Consumer debt (monthly payments)	$476
Saving/401(k)	?
Net Income	$3,500

After all this person's expenses are paid, how much can they save for retirement? Their total expenses are $2,804, leaving them with $696 left over each month. Not too shabby! First, let's see where they can cut down on spending even more. As a single person, they can trim their "Going Out" category—think restaurants, coffee, bowling alleys, and other fun stuff—by half. Next, pay off any consumer debt as quickly as possible. But even without changing their lifestyle, they can still save a good chunk. They could contribute to their 401(k) or max out their IRA contribution of $6,500 per year and still have $1,852 left over to help pay off debt or save for another goal.

Budget Like a Pro
We recommend starting your budgeting journey by reviewing once a week to get the hang of it. After a month, switch to monthly check-ins. If you're married, your spouse should join these budget meetings to understand the household financial situation. Give yourself some grace—most people won't get the budget right immediately. Money experts like Suze Orman say it may take about three months to get your budget where it needs to be.

BECOMING A 401(K) MILLIONAIRE

Focus on Savings

In addition to saving, focus on where you put that money. A 401(k) or other employer-sponsored retirement savings plan is a great place to start, thanks to the tax-deductible contributions, tax-deferred growth, and ease of management. There are other options for retirement savings, but a 401(k) is hard to beat, especially if your employer matches your contributions. It's a no-brainer!

Investing Wisely: Choosing the Right Funds

When it comes to investing, choosing where to put your dollars is crucial. I highly recommend a low-cost, institutionally managed investment portfolio through a company like Vanguard, Schwab, or Fidelity. I've mentioned Vanguard throughout this book for a reason. Finding a trusted fund family in which to invest your capital with minimal barriers to your success is essential. We suggest these funds for their low costs, global diversification, and decreasing risk as you near retirement. Most low-cost index funds focusing on the S&P 500 or the total market are wise choices. For those who can handle some volatility, investing in stocks can maximize long-term asset growth. While stocks are more volatile, combining them with safer personal savings, a company match, and tax-deferred growth can boost your retirement portfolio.

Review and Adjust: Keep the Momentum

After a few months, if you find you can spare a bit more, go for it! Review that budget at least once a year to see if you can up your savings game. Here's a pro tip: you'll never meet a 50-year-old who regrets saving too much. It's usually the opposite! I learned this early on, and it's been a lifesaver. So start now, and future you will be eternally grateful.

A Personal Story: The Cost of Prioritizing Poorly

When I first graduated from school, I was driving a beat-up Ford Ranger. It was the truck I used during the summer when painting houses to help pay for college. My parents sold it to me for cheap after I graduated. I was in a new job as a financial advisor and recently married, and for some reason, we thought that getting a new car should be at the top of our list. A new car was a fine choice, but the priority I placed on that discretionary purchase instead of prioritizing retirement saving ended up costing me several thousand dollars of missed investment returns.

I'm telling my own story here but could easily be telling hundreds of other people's stories, because I see this situation a lot. For whatever reason, a new car is the first thing college graduates look to buy within two years of graduation. Maybe it's their sign of success, or maybe they really need a new car. For most, it is an extremely poor choice and one that will cost them a lot more than they think. And it all points back to saving early in life.

The Power of Saving Early versus Later

The data on saving early versus late is pretty staggering. Take, for example, the investor who started saving at 25 versus the investor who puts off saving to buy the new car and spend her new riches from a new job. Investor A puts $5,000 to work each year in a 401(k) for 10 years at an 8 percent rate of return and doesn't put in another nickel after age 35. Investor B delays investing in her 401(k) until 35 and then saves $5,000 per year for the next 25 years. Let's assume Investor B invests at the same rate of return as Investor A.

In the end, Investor A has put $50,000 to work in a 401(k) and has more than $615,000 saved at age 60. Investor B, who started later and saved $125,000 over 25 years, will end up with a little more than $430,000. This might not seem to make sense, but the numbers really do work out. Investor A saved $75,000 less than Investor B but ended up with $185,000 more at age 60. My friends, these numbers really put into perspective the benefit of saving early over waiting. Investor A experienced the power of accumulation by starting early. Most people look at it as straight-line math and forget about the compounding or that snowball we discussed earlier.

Unfortunately, Investor B represents how most people approach saving within their retirement accounts. To top it off, many like Investor B put the new car in the category of need instead of want—and 401(k) savings into want instead of need. Although I erred in buying the new car, I must give credit to the human resources person who asked me after a review how much I would like to put in my 401(k). That simple question helped change the trajectory of my financial life because that was the point at which I started purposefully saving for retirement. In a similar way, I hope that I am helping you do that for yourself right now.

Accumulation, the 401(k) Account, and Index Investing

To reiterate some of my thoughts about how to manage your 401(k) and retirement savings, consider the following: (1) accumulate the dollars you'll need for retirement over the long term, (2) save early and often, and (3) rebalance your account no more than annually.

Next, within a 401(k), it is key to buy low-cost index funds to keep more of your dollars in your account, to have a smoother ride, and to minimize the need to switch investments all the time.

There is much to be said about index investing, particularly inside a 401(k) plan. We often ask, "Can a person beat the stock market's returns over a long period of time?" My answer: "Yes, but the odds are slim, mainly because of investor behavior and the management expense you incur in trying to outperform." The odds of really being able to ride the market's ups and downs and hold tight through an investment cycle, let alone a lifetime, are tough for many 401(k) participants and investors alike. So what is the best way to invest within a 401(k) or other investment account on a consistent basis? Without hesitation, I would recommend a low-cost index fund.

The DOL recommends that those putting a retirement plan together at the company level "defray reasonable plan costs," which includes the cost of investing. It is simple, really: reduce the overall cost to invest so that those investing will keep more of what they earn. Again, investing in low-cost index funds is one of the best ways to keep more of what you contribute while benefiting from the compounding growth in the market over decades.

Consider this: comparing the average fund expense ratio at Vanguard, at a mere 0.18 percent, with the industry average, which is more than 1 percent, an investor starting with $50,000 in the Vanguard fund option will save around $60,000 in fees over a lifetime, compared to the non-Vanguard fund option. This is a difference of an extra few thousand dollars a year over 30 years, and my guess is that you have more pressing expenses during retirement than to pay a mutual fund company several thousand dollars more per year than is necessary. Regardless of how much you invest, taking the low-cost index approach when attempting to accumulate retirement dollars can provide a real growth opportunity to those who follow this path.

Investment Strategies: Options for Every Investor

When placing money in these low-cost index funds, there are several approaches from which you can choose. I will outline three of the most followed investment alternatives for retirement account investors.

Target Date Retirement Fund: The first option is the target retirement fund. As a reminder from previous chapters, the target date on the fund corresponds with the approximate date the person turns 65 (i.e., retirement age). A 50-year-old, if she were investing today, would opt for a Vanguard Target Retirement 2035 fund. These target-date funds work in a way that changes the mix of investments within the fund to become more conservative over time, gliding toward that conservative approach the closer the investor gets to retirement.

The glide path feature of target retirement funds is a blessing to investors in many ways. One of the biggest positives is that investors rarely change their investment allocations after making their initial investment selection. One internal study offered by a large mutual fund company placed the percentage of investors that invest and never change their initial investment selection at 80 percent. When viewing this practically, we see an investor's effort between the ages of 22 and 50 to invest in funds that will save and accumulate for retirement looks a lot different than the investor looking to reduce risk for retirement. The Vanguard target date retirement funds not only automatically transition an investor to a more conservative approach; they can also be a great way to minimize the risk against a big downturn in the market that would otherwise threaten the timing of one's plans to retire.

Constant Risk: Another option, which also involves our friends at Vanguard, is one based on risk. Regardless of age, if you identify yourself as a conservative investor, you may want to invest 50 percent or less of your portfolio in stocks. Conversely, if you identify with being a risk-taker and are comfortable with volatility, then a portfolio made up entirely of stocks might be the way to go. This approach differs from the target-date fund approach because the target-date fund becomes more conservative the closer you get to 65. Instead, the risk-based approach has a constant speed that is fast, medium, or slow, and it doesn't change unless you desire to shift gears and increase or decrease the speed.

Remember that with a change in speed, you also receive a corresponding increase or decrease in volatility and earning potential. As I mentioned earlier, this is the option I personally use for my wife and myself, as we are not risk averse and are therefore invested 100 percent in the stock market with no bonds.

Own Your Age in Bonds: One final approach to consider is from the Vanguard founder John Bogle himself. I have heard him say to investors, "Own your age in bonds." This acts as a modified target-date fund approach because the closer you get to retirement, the more conservative the portfolio becomes (although, the same 80-year-old in a target date fund would own approximately 30% stocks and 70% bonds). John Bogle's approach becomes progressively more conservative well beyond 65. For example, an 80-year-old investor would own 80 percent of bonds with the remaining 20 percent of his portfolio in stocks. Although I don't recommend this approach to clients, I do appreciate the wisdom of its source.

The 2020s: Navigating High Interest and Inflation

From Low Rates to High Stakes
One of the reasons I was motivated to write a second edition of *Becoming a 401(k) Millionaire* is recent factors of

interest and inflation. From the early 2000s to 2020, interest rates and inflation were at rock bottom. When I wrote the first edition of this book in 2018, they were historically low. But now, in 2023, home mortgage rates are flirting with 7 to 8 percent, and inflation is bouncing between 9 and 15 percent, depending on which metric or media network you look at. Let's tackle the bad news first.

The Economic Roller Coaster
Usually, during wild economic events like COVID-19, military conflicts in Eastern Europe and the Middle East, and soaring inflation, stocks take a bigger hit than bonds. But surprise! Bonds have tanked more than expected. While stocks dipped in 2021 and 2022, they've managed to claw back to new highs. Typically, people turn to bonds for safety during unpredictable times. But today, long-term bonds have been hit hard and yield less than short-term bonds. The technical term for this occurrence, when longer-term bonds pay investors less than short-term bonds, is the "inverted yield curve."

Let's dive into the mysterious world of the inverted yield curve. Don't worry, I'll keep it fun and easy to understand! For those who want to check out at the first sign of academic jargon, this is your opportunity to skip a few paragraphs. However, for those looking to wow their friends at the next summer barbecue or impress their parents over your holiday break, read on.

What's a Yield Curve Anyway?
First things first: What's a yield curve? Imagine you're at a concert, and you can either buy tickets in advance (long-term) or right at the door (short-term). Normally, buying in advance is cheaper because it's a bit of a gamble—you don't know if you'll still want to go or if something better will come up. So the longer you wait, the more you might have to pay.

In finance, it works kind of the same way with bonds. Short-term bonds (like your at-the-door ticket) usually have lower interest rates because there's less risk. Long-term bonds (your advance ticket) usually have higher rates because there's more uncertainty over time. If you plot these rates on a graph from short-term to long-term, you get a yield curve.

The Normal Curve versus the Weird One
In a "normal" world, the yield curve slopes up—higher rates for long-term bonds and lower rates for short-term ones. But sometimes, this curve gets flipped on its head, like if you had to pay more for advance tickets than last-minute ones. This topsy-turvy situation is called an **inverted yield curve**.

When does this happen? An inverted yield curve happens when short-term interest rates become higher than long-term rates. Think of it like a crazy day where concert organizers decide you should pay more if you want the uncertainty of an advance ticket and less for the guarantee of getting in right away.

Why does this happen? This flipping usually happens because investors are worried about the future. They think the economy might tank soon, so they want the safety of long-term investments, even if they get lower returns. They buy up long-term bonds, driving those prices up and yields down (remember, price and yield move in opposite directions). Meanwhile, short-term bond yields rise because investors aren't as interested in them.

The Big Deal: A Recession Indicator
Why should you care? Well, the inverted yield curve has a spooky reputation for predicting recessions. It's like the finance world's version of a bad omen. When short-term rates are higher than long-term ones, it often means people are expecting bad times ahead, and historically, this has often led to an economic downturn.

Putting It All Together
So, to recap:

1. **Yield Curve**: Shows interest rates from short-term to long-term bonds

2. **Normal Yield Curve**: Slopes up (higher rates for long-term bonds)

3. **Inverted Yield Curve**: Flips upside down (higher rates for short-term bonds)

4. **Why It Inverts**: Investors fear the future and flock to long-term bonds. The excess volume of purchases drives rates down

5. **Why It Matters**: Often signals a recession might be coming

And there you have it! The inverted yield curve, explained in a way that (hopefully) makes sense and maybe even brought a smile to your face. Keep an eye out for it—it's one of those quirky financial phenomena that can tell us a lot about what might be coming next.

The Silver Lining
The Federal Reserve has been hiking interest rates to combat inflation and unemployment. The bright side? Conservative investments like savings accounts, CDs, and treasury bonds are now offering decent returns. Some savings accounts are flaunting 4 percent interest, and CDs are hitting 5 percent. Plus, as of January 2023, the S&P 500 has regained some ground. This might change by the time you're reading this, so don't hold me to it!

Inflation: The Unwelcome Guest
Now for some unwelcome news: inflation is sky-high, eating away at gains in any investment type. Beating 9 to 15 percent inflation is no easy feat. Few investments can outpace that, though real estate and some businesses might have a shot. The best move right now? Don't panic. Pay off variable consumer debt first, as those interest rates are

skyrocketing. Remember, every credit card has a variable interest rate. If possible, keep investing and snag that 401(k) match. This crazy inflation won't last forever, so grab any extra money you can get.

If you're struggling, find ways to boost your income. Ask for a raise, take on extra hours, pick up additional tasks for more pay, get a second job, or start a side hustle. Anything to bring in more money will help you combat inflation. And don't forget to revisit your budget. Groceries have been hit hard by inflation. Where can you cut back to improve your financial situation?

In Conclusion

Even with all this chaos, don't stop investing in your 401(k). You've set a strategy, and now more than ever, you need to stick to it. Don't let the noise distract you from what you can control.

Choosing to save early and often can help undo many investment mistakes. Overcoming market fears and maintaining a more aggressive investment stance can significantly boost your portfolio's ending balance. Managing costs, though second to saving early and often, can help you keep more of what you earn for retirement. Many will try to dip into their hard-earned retirement money, so if there's a time to be stingy, it's now.

You now have many tools of knowledge to use as a wise investor. Putting these tools to work is one of the best ways to build your retirement nest egg. So get out there and start making those smart financial moves!

Key Points from Chapter 4

1. **Start Saving Early:** The earlier you start saving for retirement, the more you'll benefit from compound interest. Starting at a younger age allows your investments more time to grow, significantly increasing your retirement savings compared to starting later in life.

2. **Create and Maintain a Budget**: Establishing a budget helps you determine how much you can afford to save. Regularly reviewing and adjusting your budget can help you find additional savings opportunities and ensure you're maximizing your retirement contributions.

3. **Prioritize Retirement Savings**: Making retirement savings a priority, even over discretionary spending like buying a new car, can have a substantial impact on your financial future. Small sacrifices now can lead to significant rewards later.

4. **Invest in Low-Cost Index Funds**: Choosing low-cost, institutionally managed investment portfolios, such as those offered by Vanguard, can help you keep more of your money. These funds typically offer global diversification and lower fees, which can lead to higher returns over time.

5. **Understand the Power of Stocks**: Investing heavily in stocks during your prime accumulation years (ages 22 to 55) can yield higher returns compared to more conservative investments like bonds. While stocks are more volatile, their long-term growth potential makes them a crucial component of a robust retirement portfolio.

6. **Rebalance Your Portfolio Annually**: Regularly rebalancing your portfolio ensures that your investments align with your risk tolerance and retirement goals. This practice helps maintain the desired asset allocation and minimizes the impact of market fluctuations.

7. **Stick to Your Investment Plan During Economic Uncertainty**: High inflation and interest rates can create financial challenges, but it's important to stay the course with your investment strategy. Avoid making emotional decisions and focus on long-term goals to navigate economic volatility successfully.

CHAPTER 5

THE POWER OF SMALL DECISIONS

For many, a little knowledge can go a long way, or as one Old Testament writer put it, "My people are destroyed for lack of knowledge." Maybe we're not talking destruction in the same way Hosea conceived it, but a person and their family can do their part today to avoid financial destruction by making a habit of saving. Remind yourself as you spend $4 a day on your favorite coffee that it's not just the cost of the drink that's the killer; it's the lost opportunity of what those dollars could become if they were invested and growing tax-free for the next 40 years.

The Power of Small Sacrifices

Saving does not have to be an all-or-nothing proposition. Skip your favorite $4 drink half the time and do that for 40 years, and you save nearly $30,000, and by investing those dollars, you'll create a nest egg of more than $380,000.

Look at that drink, that extra subscription, that club membership, and so forth, and think to yourself, "How important are those things relative to saving for retirement?"

Because you have taken the time to read this book, I hope you are thinking differently about this now. If more investors and savers knew that $4 spent today on a coffee drink compounded to hundreds, even thousands, of dollars over a working lifetime, it might cause them to pause before the purchase.

Debt-Free Investing

I have hinted at this in previous chapters, but I want to make it clear that if you are struggling with consumer debt (credit cards, auto loans, many "hard money" loans, etc.), you need to focus on paying off that debt first. Consumer debt often involves high, and sometimes variable, interest rates. As of 2023, Americans have amassed over a trillion dollars in *both* student loans and credit cards. Interest rates on these loans range from 4 percent to 28 percent or higher. Very few investments can make more than that to make the math work. I want to encourage you to be consumer debt free before investing in your retirement accounts.

If you get into debt and you are already investing in your retirement accounts, you may want to consider ceasing contributions and focus on bringing your consumer debt load to zero. Life happens, and sometimes you may need that extra cash flow to finance a medical emergency or mechanic bill. Pay off everything but the mortgage before deciding to invest for retirement. Ideally, you should have your house paid off before you decide to retire and start drawing from your retirement accounts.

The Balance Between Spending and Saving

I hope the takeaway from this book is not "Do not spend" while saving and investing most everything into your retirement account. That is not my intent. What I do hope is that savers and investors put as much focus on saving and investing for retirement as they do on spending. Or how about this? Spend half the time you devote to browsing social media, watching Netflix, and catching the game, and invest in learning more about financial planning, which includes disciplines like saving, investing, and budgeting. I am not saying that a trip to Disneyland is bad, nor is binge watching a season of your favorite show. But if you have spent more time planning your trip to Disneyland or crushing the latest Netflix series than you have planned for retirement, that is an issue. Seriously.

What if you were to forgo your next trip to Disneyland and instead use that money to buy Disney stock? Let's say you were planning on spending $5,000 on a trip to Disneyland in 2002 but instead, you bought DIS (NYSE) at $15 per share. Today, 15 years later, those 330 shares would be worth more than $30,000. A little saved today can pay for years' worth of trips to Disneyland; it's just a matter of thinking and spending a little differently. Or, what if instead of another hour of swiping on Instagram, you were to go to a trusted financial resource and learn a thing or two? Anyone can do this with just about any purchase. And anyone can delegate a portion of time they are already spending online to learning about retirement.

Begin thinking now. Begin learning and researching now. This is not only about retirement but also about paying for future purchases of things you like. Look at your total spending on coffee; commit next year to spend half that amount on coffee and invest the other half in Starbucks stock. If you're a tractor buyer, put off the purchase of another tractor for a year or two and instead buy John Deere stock. I've watched clients do this for years, and it works. Whether saving money in a 401(k), an IRA, or a 403(b), it is about saving for a future spending need—be it retirement or future tractors and coffee.

Thinking Long-Term

The point I want you to take away is that the small, everyday decisions add up to major differences in the long term. Certainly, there is a lot more to life than money and planning for retirement. But even though retirement saving is probably not at the top of anyone's list, it is a huge issue that deserves more attention than it gets. There is a small portion of society that has saved well. But this cannot be an exclusive club. Healthy retirement account balances must be a venue where everyone has access and success.

My hope is that you will apply what you have learned to make optimal choices in how you spend, where you decide to work, how to take advantage of your 401(k) plan, and what sort of investments are best for you. In doing so, you will have a great answer to the question of "How you are going to support yourself and your family when you are no longer working?" You can say you are on your way to becoming the next 401(k) millionaire.

Key Points from Chapter 5

1. **The Impact of Small Sacrifices:** Small, consistent savings, like skipping a $4 coffee daily, can accumulate to significant amounts over time. Investing these small amounts can grow into a substantial nest egg due to the power of compounding.

2. **Importance of Knowledge:** A lack of financial knowledge can lead to poor financial decisions. Understanding the long-term benefits of saving and investing is crucial to avoiding financial pitfalls and achieving financial security.

3. **Prioritize Debt Repayment:** Before focusing on investing, prioritize paying off high-interest consumer debt such as credit cards and student loans. The high interest rates on those debts often outweigh potential investment returns.

4. **Balance Spending and Saving:** It's essential to find a balance between enjoying life now and saving for the future. While spending on experiences like trips to Disneyland can create great memories, it's also important to plan and save for long-term financial stability.

5. **Investing in Stocks:** Redirecting funds from discretionary spending to investments, like buying shares in companies you frequently purchase from, can yield significant returns over time.

6. **State of American Savings:** Half of Americans have saved nothing for retirement. Do what is in your power to save now and save often.

7. **Long-Term Thinking:** Adopting a long-term perspective on saving and investing can lead to better financial outcomes. Consistent, disciplined investing over many years, even with small amounts, can significantly improve financial security in retirement.

CHAPTER 6

THE POWER OF THE 401(K) AND THE REALITY OF SOCIAL SECURITY

There are two primary reasons to save for retirement: (1) you'll need income-producing assets when you no longer have a paycheck from your job, and (2) Social Security is not the retirement dream that some think. In this chapter, I want to highlight how the 401(k) has become the retirement savings vehicle of choice in the United States while underscoring the state of Social Security and how it fits into a retirement plan. I hope tracing this history will help you understand even better the indispensable role that the 401(k) plays in ensuring a successful retirement today.

401(k) History: From Pensions to Personal Savings

The rise of the 401(k) plan can be attributed to both the inherent limitations of traditional pension plans and the

DR. PETER FISHER

broader economic challenges of the late 1970s. Traditional pension plans impose significant financial burdens on employers, primarily due to the guaranteed income promised to retirees, the unpredictability of investment returns, fluctuating interest rates, and the uncertain lifespan of beneficiaries. These factors made pension plans increasingly untenable for many companies.

In the 1970s the US economy grappled with severe issues such as soaring inflation, which peaked at 13.3 percent in 1979, and sluggish economic growth, with negative GDP growth in 1974 and 1975. The oil crises of 1973 and 1979 further exacerbated economic instability, leading to high unemployment rates; these rates reached 8.2 percent in 1975. Such economic conditions, combined with the shifting dynamics of the workforce, underscored the need for a more flexible and less burdensome retirement savings option, paving the way for the widespread adoption of 401(k) plans.

Before 1978 most companies offered retirement benefits through company-funded pension plans. When I started in the financial services industry in the mid-1990s, it was fairly common for these pensions to be part of a client's retirement plan. Customers with a company pension enjoyed many benefits, including guaranteed lifetime income, professional management, predictable planning, and cost-of-living adjustments. When paired with their Social Security benefits, a company pension plan allowed individuals to retire with little worry and stable paychecks.

The Shift from Pensions to 401(k)s

While company-sponsored pension plans offered a stable source of income for retirees, they faced significant challenges. One major drawback was the required length of service before receiving any benefits, often necessitating 10, 20, or even 30 years of employment with the same company. Additionally, pensions lacked portability. Unlike modern retirement plans, where individuals can leave their funds with their employer, roll them into an IRA, or transfer them to a new employer's 401(k), the company controls pension plans. This lack of portability was particularly problematic if the company faced financial difficulties, leaving employees' retirement funds at risk.

In certain instances, financial difficulties compelled companies to file for bankruptcy, leading them to terminate their pension plans. Upon declaring bankruptcy, these pensions were transferred to the Pension Benefit Guaranty Corporation (PBGC). In the United States, the PBGC serves as a safeguard for failed company pension plans. This transition was highly stressful for employees, often resulting in reduced benefit payments, significantly impacting their retirement lifestyle.

By 1978 the conditions were ideal for a major shift in how American workers funded their retirement. The economic challenges of the time, coupled with the financial instability of many employers and a growing desire to give employees greater control over their retirement savings, demanded a change in retirement benefits. The crucial legislative shift came with the Revenue Act of 1978, which included a provision in the Internal Revenue Code allowing employees to defer a portion of their salary, thereby postponing taxation on that income until it was received in the future.

The Birth of the 401(k)

In 1980 benefits consultant Ted Benna ingeniously interpreted this provision and proposed a plan enabling employees to contribute pretax dollars into a retirement account, with the possibility of an employer match. This innovative concept gained momentum when the IRS confirmed that employers could legally defer a portion of an employee's paycheck into a retirement savings account. As a result, major companies, including the Johnson Companies and Pepsi, began offering these 401(k) accounts as a significant employee benefit. Today, these accounts are a cornerstone of retirement planning for many workers.

Social Security: A Safety Net with Holes

As I've previewed, one thing I want you to keep in mind as you anticipate retirement is the precarious state of Social Security. Let me explain why I think this is important.

The Social Security Administration (SSA) is an independent agency of the United States federal government responsible for administering Social Security. This social insurance program includes retirement, disability, and survivor benefits. Social Security was established on August 14, 1935, when President Franklin D. Roosevelt signed the Social Security Act into law. The primary aim of the program was to provide financial assistance to the elderly, who were hit hardest during the Great Depression, which began in 1929 and left millions of Americans unemployed and impoverished. Many elderly people had no savings or reliable source of income, leading to widespread poverty among this demographic. The Social Security program was designed to create a safety net, ensuring that retired workers would have some financial support.

Initially, Social Security was intended to benefit retired workers aged 65 or older. It provided monthly cash benefits financed through payroll taxes on both employers and employees. This was a significant shift, as it established a federal government role in providing income security for the elderly. Over time, the program has expanded to include benefits for disabled individuals, survivors of deceased workers, and the dependents of beneficiaries, making it a cornerstone of the American social safety net.

To be sure, Social Security is far from a full retirement benefit. A recent review of data from the Social Security Administration showed that the average benefit for a retired worker was $1,909.01. Think about $1,909 within the context of rent or a car payment. It's hard to imagine the average American being able to live a quality retirement on that amount. Certainly, there are plenty of individuals receiving more than $1,900. Moreover, plenty of individuals can live comfortably on $1,900 per month. But for most, Social Security falls short of the retirement dream. Importantly, because Social Security is grossly underfunded, there is a chance (without changes) that Social Security benefits after 2035 will be discounted.

DR. PETER FISHER

The Dire Shape of Social Security
What do Social Security's financial challenges mean for you and your future? The shortfall is primarily due to demographic shifts, including the aging of the Baby Boomer generation, increased life expectancy, and a declining birth rate, which results in fewer workers paying into the system relative to the number of beneficiaries. If the trust funds are exhausted, Social Security can only pay about 83 percent of scheduled benefits from ongoing tax revenues.

Without reform, Social Security's future is uncertain. Potential solutions to ensure its solvency include increasing payroll taxes, raising the retirement age, adjusting the benefits formula, or a combination of these measures. However, political gridlock has made it challenging to implement any significant changes. For individuals planning their retirement, it's crucial to consider the potential impact of these financial issues on their benefits and to diversify their retirement savings strategies beyond relying solely on Social Security.

Planning for a Future without Social Security
The critical issue is not whether funds will be available by 2035 but rather whether you should rely on Social Security as a significant component of your retirement income. The key takeaway is Social Security should not be considered a substantial part of your retirement planning, regardless of age. Nevertheless, some individuals can rely on Social Security and benefit from it. Here are a few scenarios to consider for your retirement planning:

- **A 58-year-old individual** who has worked since age 21 and plans to retire at 62 could live on Social Security benefits, receiving approximately $3,200 per month.

- **A 50-year-old person** who did not work full-time for most of their adult life and intends to retire at 65 may need to reassess their retirement plans, as they cannot depend on Social Security alone.

- **Almost any young person under the age of 50** (including those in their 40s) will need to finance their own retirement, as Social Security will not provide sufficient income for a comfortable retirement.

This situation may seem unfair, and I share that sentiment, but we cannot rely on an impending act of Congress to resolve it. Personally, I prefer to take control of what I can manage and let Congress handle its own affairs.

No Social Security? No Problem! 401(k) by the Numbers

The vehicle of choice for most successful retirement savers is the 401(k)—and it might be the best savings vehicle of all time. There are several reasons I am compelled to make such a bold statement. The benefits of a 401(k) are multifold: tax-deductible contributions, tax-free growth, matching (if your employer offers it), and dollar-cost averaging of your investment (which, in short, allows an investor to accumulate more shares with the same dollars at lower price points, thus lowering the average cost per share to purchase). Each of these 401(k) attributes plays a significant role in helping you retire.

There is no habit too important or luxury worth having that ought to come before saving for retirement. Building wealth in your retirement account will help you not have to depend on others, grant you freedom, and give more time for things you are passionate about. We will discuss some behavioral finance topics in a later chapter that will give you insight on how you can tackle the issue of not wanting to save.

Traditional versus Roth 401(k)

For traditional 401(k) contributions, the tax-deductible contribution is a huge benefit. And the goodness doesn't stop there. One of the attributes of both traditional 401(k) accounts and Roth 401(k) accounts is the tax-deferred growth of the investments. For investors outside a 401(k) account, there are a variety of taxes and rates one pays for short- and long-term gains, in addition to dividends and interest. For investors who defer dollars into a 401(k), whether with pre-tax (traditional) or after-tax dollars (Roth), the tax-deferred compounding effect can be significant.

If you are not sure which one to choose, it is usually best to start with a Roth 401(k) and eventually transition to a traditional if you wanted to. When you start working in your career, your income is typically lower than it ever will be, and at this point, your income tax bracket is low so your after-tax contributions into your Roth will be lower than when you withdraw from your 401(k) later. But if you just started to invest and you are in a high-income tax bracket, you may want to consider a traditional account so that you can take advantage of the tax-deductible contributions. Plus, when you retire, your income will come down so when you do withdraw from your 401(k), your income will be at the lowest it has ever been in your career.

Compare these two examples: Susan, a 22-year-old teacher, decides to open a Roth 401(k) at her private school. She makes $32,000 per year, so this is a wise choice because her income bracket is low at this point in her life. Over time, as her income rises, she may want to consider switching. Samantha, a 42-year-old engineer, has not opened a retirement account yet, but she just read this book and wants to tap into her company's 401(k). Her income is $150,000 per year, so she would do best to take advantage of a traditional 401(k) so she can lower her taxable income with her contributions and take advantage of the company match. When she retires, she may only need to withdraw $32,000 per year, which is much lower than her highest income, so her tax bill will not be that bad.

Conclusion

I hope after you read this book that you will see it as a no-brainer to have a little less in your pocket at the end of the month in an effort to secure a decent retirement for yourself and your family. And this is just the beginning of the financial benefit. The next benefit is that by investing those funds, you will watch them grow tax-free. Any chance you get to take a tax break in this life, you should take it. The less money you give to the government in taxes, the more money you can keep to advance your family's financial position or give to charity.

As I have told many individuals over the years, a 401(k) is the optimal place to save. For those who don't believe me, I challenge you to come up with a better way. If you can find one that allows for tax-deductible contributions, tax-free growth, the ease of payroll deductions, and the possibility of a company match, go for it—and let me know about your findings (my email is at the end of the book)! If not, sign up for your company's 401(k) and make the most of it. You won't regret it.

Key Points from Chapter 6

1. **Importance of Saving for Retirement:** Relying solely on Social Security for retirement is risky due to potential fund depletion by 2035. Saving and investing through a 401(k) can provide financial security and independence in retirement.

2. **History of the 401(k):** The 401(k) was introduced in 1978 as part of the Revenue Act, signed by President Jimmy Carter. It replaced traditional company-funded pension plans, offering employees a new way to save for retirement through tax-deferred contributions.

3. **Limitations of Social Security:** Social Security is projected to only be able to pay 83 percent of scheduled benefits after 2035. Relying solely on

Social Security for retirement is not advisable, especially for those under 50, who should prioritize personal savings and investments.

4. **Benefits of a 401(k):** The 401(k) offers several advantages, including tax-deductible contributions, tax-free growth, employer matching, and dollar-cost averaging. These benefits can significantly enhance retirement savings over time.

5. **Tax-Deductible Contributions:** Contributions to a traditional 401(k) reduce taxable income, allowing for more money to be invested and grow over time. This tax advantage can result in substantial savings and growth compared to a regular savings account.

6. **Choosing Between the Traditional and Roth 401(k):** The decision depends on current and expected future income. Young professionals with lower income may benefit more from a Roth 401(k), while higher earners may find a traditional 401(k) more advantageous due to immediate tax deductions.

7. **Long-Term Growth Potential:** Consistent contributions to a 401(k) over 30 years, with a balanced investment strategy, can lead to significant growth. For example, saving $4,320 annually can potentially grow to over $500,000, demonstrating the power of compounding and tax-deferred growth.

CHAPTER 7

FLIPPING THE SWITCH: FROM SAVER TO SPENDER IN RETIREMENT

Embracing Retirement

For those of you reading this book in your 60s or early 70s, or anyone contemplating retirement for that matter, your first day of retirement is a huge day—maybe as big as the day you decided to forgo those optional luxuries and contribute to your retirement account! This transition can be a terrifying time as you look at your accounts and see how they have grown but don't know how to flip the switch from retirement saver to retirement spender. It's also nerve-racking because mistakes might derail the flush retirement you envisioned. Still, the fact that you're reading this book means you've taken a major step toward being prepared. You've got this.

For those of you in the retirement accumulation phase of life, say 22 to 52, do not discount this chapter. You will want to understand how to retire well and what that might look like. Understanding these concepts now can set you up for a smoother transition when your time comes.

Consider Shawna, who came to my firm with a troubling situation. She had recently retired after teaching her entire life. Because insurance companies and their brokers are allowed in schools to offer tax-sheltered annuities (TSAs), she willingly met with one of the agents she had become familiar with over the years. Unfortunately, she took his counsel and rolled her pension into an annuity account, leaving behind all the guaranteed income, cost-of-living adjustments, and security that came with it. I will discuss annuities and why you should not invest in them later in this chapter.

All this to say, Shawna's story went from bad to worse when the lofty projections the agent had presented to her didn't materialize because the timing of her investments was poor. By the time Shawna contacted us, she was hip-deep in a lawsuit and looking to clean up her remaining balances.

Although this example is extreme, things like this can happen without careful planning and a team of good people around you to advise you at retirement and beyond. So what do you do when you are considering retirement or beginning the process? Here are some steps to help you avoid similar pitfalls:

Step 1: Assemble Your Retirement Dream Team
Put together a team of advisors and come up with a game plan. If you do not have an advisor, I recommend interviewing several individuals referred to you by people you trust. Ask them for their credentials—this is critical. Later in this chapter, we will discuss what specific credentials you should be looking for.

Step 2: Vet Your Potential Advisors
Ask these potential advisors for lists of their services, how they are paid, if they are fiduciaries (people who hold a legal or ethical relationship of trust with one or more parties—typically, a fiduciary prudently takes care of money or other assets for another person), what their investment track records have been, and so forth. Next, check them out online, but not on their website, because their marketing department put that together for them to look good. Track down their information on the internet by typing "advisor check" and each name into a browser and looking at that information, which is required by law to be disclosed.

Reading customer complaints and settlements can offer an early warning of issues to come. A ding on an advisor's record could be similar to a speeding ticket received by someone who is not normally a fast driver. However, if there are repeated issues with an advisor you are considering, particularly within the past few years, beware.

Step 3: Evaluate Their Recommendations
The idea of this advisor search is that once you have selected an advisor or taken the time to see what your advisor

or team recommends, you will be able to consider their recommendation within the context of a financial plan. I cannot stress enough how important this is. Working with a Certified Financial Planner (CFP©) who has a team around them and top-notch planning software is a solid approach when it comes to looking at retirement projections.

Be certain to look at the assumptions that have been made when putting together your plan. As an example, rate of return assumptions and inflation expectations can have a huge impact on returns. If you don't like the recommendations your advisor is giving you based on the various assumptions, ask questions about how things are adding up behind the scenes and take the time to understand it. In addition to plan assumptions, pay attention to whether the advisor is factoring in their fee when considering your retirement budget. All these things can have a huge impact on you and your ability to retire.

By following these steps and building a strong team, you can avoid many of the pitfalls that people like Shawna have faced. The right planning and guidance can make all the difference in achieving the secure and comfortable retirement you envision.

Mapping Your Journey to Financial Success

Financial planning is the process of organizing and managing your money to help reach your goals. There are many parts of financial planning that advisors can assist you on:

- Budgeting, saving, and debt management

- Taxes and accounting

- Investing advice

- Helping you with long-term goals like retirement and education planning

- Insurance guidance

- Assisting with private pursuits like businesses or philanthropy

You can get either partial help in these categories for a temporary time or a comprehensive plan that covers all these categories and is usually a long-term commitment.

Ed's Story: Choosing the Right Advisor

Let's look at Ed, who was preparing to retire and wisely interviewed several firms to help shepherd his funds during retirement. We were fortunate to be a part of the interview process but did not end up working with Ed. In the interview process, a competing firm showed him a retirement outcome that was much more favorable than ours. The rate-of-return assumptions were similar, but the inflation expectations and the expected rate of return of the bond portion of his portfolio were much more aggressive than we felt comfortable using, given Ed's age and need for income.

As a result, the competitor's plan looked much better because the inflation numbers were a percentage point lower and the bond returns were several percentage points higher. We gave Ed what we thought was a realistic picture based on his situation, but we lost the opportunity to serve him. We aren't sure if Ed chose a firm that was a nonfiduciary, but we do know they did not serve his best interest. The takeaway here is that it's essential to understand the differences in recommendations. Asking why the numbers are different, or asking for the underlying assumptions, can lead you to a better outcome.

The Fiduciary Standard: Putting Clients First

Fiduciary firms like mine will focus on how to serve you best first. Fiduciaries will focus on realistic numbers and outcomes as they pertain to your financial situation and your goals. Some financial advisors will advertise great returns if you go into business with them. This is fine and legal to do, but do not let these numbers distract you from your plan and goals. Just like any business, these advisors post high projected numbers to bring in new clients.

The job of an advisor should not be to get business but to do excellent work in advising their clients. This, in fact, is the fiduciary standard—to have the "highest standard of care" when serving the client, not to give the client unrealistic expectations about retiring and retirement to persuade him to hire you. I cannot underscore enough how important the planning process is for a client who has his landing gear down and is ready to use the dollars from his investments.

Finding the Right Advisor

Find a great firm that uses a team approach, and ensure the team members have credentials in the areas where you need help. A few credentials to look for are Certified Financial Planner (CFP©) and Certified Public Accountant (CPA), because the decision to retire is as much about what you earn and how you earn it as it is about the tax consequences of your plan decisions. Ideally, you can find people with both credentials in the same firm.

For your reference, the list below breaks down the most common types of financial advisors and their differences:

- **CFP—Certified Financial Planner:** CFPs must pass difficult assessments, log hundreds of hours of education and real-world experience, and operate under fiduciary standards for their clients.

- **CPA—Certified Public Accountant:** CPAs are heavily regulated by private and government agencies. They are experts in taxes and accounting, and some also offer financial advice and other services. CPAs must log hundreds of hours working in their field and pass several rigorous exams, and are held to a high standard when conducting their business.

- **Financial Coach/Consultant:** These positions usually do not require formal training or national recognition. They are typically for beginners who need a starting point or low-cost guidance on financial concepts.

- **ChFC—Chartered Financial Consultant:** ChFCs must pass similar assessments and experience standards as CFPs and are also held to a fiduciary standard.

- **Wealth Advisor/Manager:** These professionals take a broad approach to building and maintaining wealth. Most financial advisors must undergo training and be regulated by private and public agencies to advise and pick investments for their clients. However, not all wealth managers or financial planners are held to a fiduciary standard, which is important to consider when selecting a financial advisor.

Doing Your Homework
Before choosing an advisor, make sure you do your homework. You should compare at least three to five advisors in your area. Interview them in person and make sure you bring a list of questions with you. You can also research financial advisors by using the following suggested resources:

- Verify a CFP® Professional | CFP Board

- Your Advisor Guide Homepage | American: Your Advisor Guide

- CPA Verify

- Check the status and reviews of the business at your local Chamber of Commerce

- Check Your Investment Professional | SEC.gov

- BBB

- Check your Community Facebook Page!

- BrokerCheck | FINRA

We can't stress enough the importance of researching several advisors before you select one. Don't go with the first one you find or one your friends and family recommend. Others' goals are different from yours.

Checking Fee Structures
While researching advisors, make sure to check fee structures. The most common types are flat fee rates for one service, charges based on the percentage of assets under management (AUM), hourly fees, and commissions. Here's a table showing the range of costs you can expect:

Fee Structure	**Cost Range**
Flat Rate	$1,000–$3,000
Percentage of AUM	0.5%–2% annually
Hourly Fee	$100–$400 per hour
Commission	Varies based on product

Rolling Over Your 401(k)

When converting your investments to a retirement posture, one of the first steps is rolling the money out of the 401(k) and into your own rollover IRA. There are exceptions to this step, but generally, a rollover IRA offers expanded investment choices and eliminates 401(k) administration costs. Your employer's HR department will have the necessary paperwork to get the process going. Most 401(k) accounts can be rolled over to a rollover IRA fairly quickly. In many cases, the investments inside your 401(k) that are being rolled over to a rollover IRA will liquidate (i.e., be sold to cash) with no tax penalty, and the funds will continue to be treated in the same tax-free and tax-deferred way they were inside your 401(k) account.

If you work with a firm like mine, you will call that firm and they will educate you on your choices and expedite the process. Keep in mind: not all companies work like ours, so the process of transferring the funds can differ.

Choosing Your Retirement Investments

Whether you decide to work with an advisor or do it yourself, knowing the expected rate of return that you will need to outpace inflation, taxes, and so forth is very important. Once you have determined what rate of earnings you will need, it is time to consider your mix of investments (i.e., portfolio). This, too, can be an incredibly tricky process, so let's break it down.

DIY versus Professional Help

If you decide to go down the do-it-yourself (DIY) path, make sure you measure the advantages and disadvantages of doing so. Here are some common reasons people choose the DIY path:

- **Wealth Threshold:** Many people simply do not have enough wealth to manage and feel they can handle their finances on their own.

- **Cost:** Financial advisors can be expensive.

- **Control:** "No one can manage your money better than you" mindset.

- **Simplicity:** No fees, no hassle, no drama, no dealing with others.

- **Trust Issues:** Trusting someone with your money is difficult.

- **Autonomy:** You are in control and making your own decisions.

As good as it seems to DIY, as with any project, there are some significant drawbacks:

- **Time:** Time spent researching, setting up accounts, planning, moving money, and other operations.

- **Effort:** The amount of effort required to set up a successful financial plan.

- **Knowledge Gap:** Not knowing what to do and potential mistakes.

- **Lower Returns:** DIYers can experience lower returns (on average) compared to people with advisors.

- **Constant Updates:** Having to continually check tax laws and investment policies.

- **Risk Understanding:** Not completely understanding risk and not having someone to ask for advice.

Avoiding Common Investment Mistakes

One of the biggest mistakes individuals going into retirement make is being overly conservative. Certainly, there should be caution heading into retirement, especially if there is no other income from other savings or investments. Most retirees cannot afford the risk of having their entire retirement savings in high-risk investments. At the same time, it would be equally outrageous to place all of an individual's savings into cash, because the effect of inflation and taxes would quickly erode it. For most of us, some portion of our portfolios needs to be invested at a rate of return that is greater than what the expected return on cash would be.

The Safe Bucket Strategy

We recommend to most of our clients keeping 3 to 5 years of investment income dollars in a "safe bucket," or cash. Why that amount? Based on my experience, if an investor has 3 to 5 years' worth of cash on hand in a banking or savings account, she doesn't tend to worry about the inevitable volatility of the stock market. We recommend creating a paycheck for the investor, so he is getting a specific amount transferred each month into his checking account. The remaining portion of his portfolio can be invested in a balanced manner (for example, 70 percent stocks and 30 percent bonds) with a focus on dividend-paying stocks and diversified bonds. For some, using this approach can add another 5 to 10 years' worth of cash flow from the dividend-paying stocks and bonds.

This safe-bucket approach has the ability to get investors to a place where they won't need to touch their stock investments for 10-plus years! This is huge for retirees who are looking to their portfolios as a main driver of income. Further, in my experience, this sort of approach is the right balance of cash, cash flow, and long-term growth, allowing retirees to live confident in having a quality lifestyle that is keeping up with inflation over their lifetimes.

What I Would Not Do with My Money

1. *Put My Money in an Annuity*

    The first thing I would not do with my money is put it in an annuity. If a retiree can take the cash they have and put together a game plan for postretirement saving and investing, there should be no need for an annuity. The bank CDs and bonds are a much more liquid and less expensive alternative to annuities. Insurance companies consistently make money on annuities by investing your capital in higher-yielding investments while paying you the equivalent of CD returns. The investor may or may not do well with annuities, but one thing is for sure—the insurance company will make out quite well. There are some instances where an annuity could possibly make sense, but they are rare, so generally, I recommend a retirement investor steer clear of annuities.

2. *Roll a Pension into Another Account*
If you will be getting a pension from your company, I would not recommend rolling it into a rollover IRA or other account. A pension is different than a 401(k). Pension dollars are guaranteed by the company and paid out over the course of an employee's retirement years. Pensions, in most cases, are as good as gold because they are guaranteed. Your company or previous employer is tasked with setting aside and investing the dollars to pay out later. Even if the monthly amount is small, consider it similar to a bond or CD, which will allow you to invest the other portion of your portfolio more aggressively, giving you a better chance of maximizing your returns over time.

I have seen some very well-put-together retirement plans using pensions, Social Security, and real estate that allow for ample cash flow and the ability to hold off taking money out of retirement accounts until absolutely needed. So do not roll over that company pension as there is likely only one winner there, and that is your insurance broker or advisor, not you.

3. *Automatically Take Social Security at Retirement*
   Finally, while you should not plan to rely solely on Social Security, do not underestimate the power of your Social Security and the strategies you can put in place to maximize retirement income. At our firm, we have CPAs and CFPs that help guide this discussion.

   I have seen how the planning process can affect Social Security decisions. More often than not, individuals go to the Social Security Administration offices and start taking Social Security with little understanding of the choices they have regarding when to start receiving these dollars. Delaying to full retirement age, 70 or older, can mean the addition of hundreds of thousands of guaranteed dollars in your pocket for the rest of your life. My recommendation is to not automatically start taking Social Security at retirement. Instead, have a plan, know your options, and see if you are able to delay receiving these dollars without additional risk to your budget. In order to maximize your benefit, you may need to work a bit longer, pick up part-time work or a consulting job, or draw on other investment assets first. In the end, looking at Social Security as an investment to be wisely turned into dollars to live on is an easy way to make a riskless, guaranteed return on your money.

Conclusion

Navigating the transition from saver to spender in retirement is no small feat, but with careful planning, the right team, and informed decisions, you can secure a comfortable and fulfilling future. Whether you're evaluating the benefits of working with a financial advisor, aiming to understand the nuances of different investment strategies, or making critical choices about Social Security and pension plans, every step is vital in building a stable retirement plan. Remember, the goal is to create a balanced approach that combines safety, growth, and a steady income stream to support your lifestyle through your golden years. By taking proactive steps now, you can avoid common pitfalls and ensure that your hard-earned savings work as efficiently for you in retirement as they did while you were accumulating them. Here's to a retirement filled with peace of mind and financial confidence!

Key Points from Chapter 7

1. **Transitioning to Retirement:** Your first day of retirement marks a significant milestone. It's essential to shift from a saver to a spender, which can be challenging without proper planning and advice. Understanding how to manage this transition is crucial for a successful retirement.

2. **Assembling a Team of Advisors:** Having a team of knowledgeable advisors, including Certified Financial Planners (CFPs) and Certified Public

Accountants (CPAs), is essential. These professionals can provide comprehensive financial planning, ensuring you make informed decisions about your retirement.

3. **The Importance of Credentials:** When you are selecting financial advisors, ensure they have the appropriate credentials and operate under fiduciary standards. This guarantees they act in your best interest and provide realistic and practical advice for your retirement planning.

4. **Avoiding Common Mistakes:** Be wary of rolling pensions into other accounts or purchasing annuities without thorough understanding and necessity. Pensions offer guaranteed income, and annuities often benefit the insurer more than the investor. Understanding these nuances can prevent costly errors.

5. **Creating a Safe Bucket:** Maintaining three to five years' worth of living expenses in cash or cash equivalents can provide a buffer against market volatility. This approach offers peace of mind as you know you have immediate funds available while allowing the rest of your portfolio to grow.

6. **Maximizing Social Security:** Strategically planning when to take Social Security can significantly impact your retirement income. Delaying benefits

until age 70 can result in a higher annual payout and a substantial cumulative increase over your lifetime.

7. **DIY versus Professional Management:** Weigh the pros and cons of managing your retirement funds yourself versus hiring a professional. While DIY can save on fees, it requires significant time, knowledge, and effort. Professionals can offer expertise and potentially higher returns, making them a valuable resource for many retirees.

PART II: THE EXPANDED FIELD OF RETIREMENT

CHAPTER 8

TAILORED RETIREMENT SOLUTIONS FOR UNIQUE SITUATIONS

This chapter is dedicated to retirement savers in various situations, such as those without access to a 401(k) at work; freelancers, self-employed individuals, contractors, and business owners; part-time or seasonal workers who do not qualify for a 401(k); low-income workers seeking a starting point; employees with poorly managed or inadequate 401(k) plans; and individuals investing in a 401(k) who want to diversify beyond this account.

While the 401(k) is a popular retirement option, it is not the only one. Think of the 401(k) as the classic black suit or dress—it's versatile and reliable, but sometimes you need to spice things up with other wardrobe choices. We will focus on a few alternative retirement accounts that can serve as excellent options for those in different employment situations.

The Rise of Nontraditional Workers

According to the Bureau of Labor Statistics, as of July 2024, 10.4 percent of working Americans are self-employed. This translates to nearly 17 million individuals who operate outside the traditional corporate structure, including freelancers, contractors, and business owners. In addition, approximately 27 million part-time workers were counted in July 2024, underscoring the significant number of people opting for alternative work arrangements.[8] With so many individuals breaking away from the typical nine-to-five grind, there's an increasing need to offer more retirement benefits to this diverse and growing group. Who knew "doing your own thing" would become the new black outfit?

Individual Retirement Accounts (IRAs)

An IRA is the easiest way to start a retirement account; anyone over 18 can open one. Typically, if you're not bringing in any income, you can't put money into a traditional or Roth IRA. However, there are exceptions for married couples filing jointly. In some cases, they can make IRA contributions based on the taxable earnings listed on their joint tax return.

IRAs do not come with employer contributions, but they offer significant advantages, such as complete control over investments and generally lower costs than 401(k)s, along with similar tax benefits.

---

8 Bureau of Labor Statistics. (2024). *Labor force statistics from the Current Population Survey*. U.S. Department of Labor. Retrieved August 5, 2024. https://data.bls.gov/pdq/SurveyOutputServlet

Let's again take a moment to compare traditional and Roth IRAs. Traditional IRAs allow contributions to be pretax, reducing taxable income, and growth is tax-free until retirement, although withdrawals are taxed as income. For example, Jane, a 30-year-old freelancer, contributes $6,000 annually to her traditional IRA, reducing her taxable income by $6,000 yearly. By the time she retires, her investments will likely grow significantly, but she will pay taxes on withdrawals based on her income bracket at retirement.

On the flip side, Roth IRAs involve after-tax contributions, meaning withdrawals in retirement are tax-free since the taxes have already been paid. For instance, Mike, a 25-year-old part-time worker, contributes $5,000 annually to his Roth IRA. He pays taxes on this income now, but when he retires, his withdrawals, including all the investment growth, will be tax-free. Imagine the freedom of taking out money without worrying about Uncle Sam's cut!

Options for Solopreneurs and Business Owners

The IRS has created incentives for self-employed individuals and business owners to save for retirement, making the road to financial freedom a little less bumpy.

A **SOLO 401(k)** is ideal for solo entrepreneurs, allowing contributions up to $66,000 in 2023. Keep in mind that business owners age 50 plus can contribute an additional "catch-up" contribution of $7,500, allowing those individuals to max out at $73,500.

SOLO 401(k)s offers a choice between traditional and Roth formats, enabling significant tax-advantaged savings.

For example, Amy, a 40-year-old solopreneur earning $250,000 annually, opens a SOLO 401(k). She contributes the maximum $66,000, significantly reducing her taxable income while growing her retirement savings tax-free. Think of it as your own personal 401(k) party, with only the best guests (your contributions) invited.

SEP IRAs (Simplified Employee Pension Individual Retirement Accounts) are a retirement savings plan primarily designed for self-employed individuals and small business owners. They provide a straightforward and tax-advantaged way to save for retirement, with several key features and benefits.

One of the main advantages of SEP IRAs is the higher contribution limits compared to traditional IRAs. As of 2023, the maximum contribution is the lesser of 25 percent of an employee's compensation or $66,000, making SEP IRAs an excellent option for those looking to save more aggressively. In these plans, only the employer contributes to the account, with the ability to contribute to their own SEP IRA and those of their eligible employees. These contributions are tax-deductible, offering significant tax benefits for the business.

SEP IRAs also have straightforward eligibility requirements: any employer, including self-employed individuals, can establish a SEP IRA. Employees must be at least 21 years old, have worked for the employer in at least three of the last five years, and have earned at least $750 in compensation during the year. Contributions to SEP IRAs are immediately 100 percent vested, meaning employees have full ownership of the funds as soon as they are made.

Employers have flexibility in making contributions and are not required to contribute yearly. They can adjust the contribution amount based on the company's financial situation. Funds in a SEP IRA grow tax-deferred, meaning taxes on investment gains are deferred until withdrawal. However, withdrawals are subject to ordinary income tax, and taking funds before age 59 1/2 may incur a 10 percent early withdrawal penalty unless an exception applies.

Let's consider an example of how contributions work for both the employer and employees in a SEP IRA: Amber owns a small marketing firm with two employees, John and Emily. In 2023, the business made a net profit of $300,000. Amber's compensation was $100,000, John's was $60,000, and Emily's was $40,000. Amber decides to contribute 10 percent of each employee's compensation to their SEP IRAs. This percentage must be consistent for all eligible employees, including Amy.

- **Amber:** 10% of $100,000 = $10,000

- **John:** 10% of $60,000 = $6,000

- **Emily:** 10% of $40,000 = $4,000

The total employer contribution amounts to $20,000. Only the employer contributes in this setup, and these contributions are fully tax-deductible. Furthermore, John and Emily's SEP IRA contributions are immediately vested, giving them full ownership of the funds immediately

SIMPLE IRAs (Savings Incentive Match Plan for Employees Individual Retirement Accounts) are retirement savings plans tailored for small businesses with 100 or fewer employees. They offer a straightforward, tax-advantaged way for both employers and employees to save for retirement. Here's an overview of the key features and benefits of SIMPLE IRAs.

Contribution Limits:
SIMPLE IRAs have lower contribution limits than SEP IRAs. As of 2023, employees can contribute up to $15,500 per year, with an additional $3,500 in catch-up contributions for those aged 50 and older. Employers are required to make contributions, either through matching contributions or nonelective contributions.

Employer Contributions:
Employers must contribute to their employees' SIMPLE IRAs, choosing one of two options:

- **Matching Contributions:** Employers match employee contributions dollar for dollar, up to 3 percent of the employee's compensation.

- **Nonelective Contributions:** Employers contribute 2 percent of each eligible employee's compensation, regardless of whether the employee contributes.

Eligibility:

The eligibility requirements for SIMPLE IRAs are minimal. Employees must have earned at least $5,000 in compensation during any two preceding years and be expected to earn at least $5,000 in the current year, making this plan accessible to a wide range of employees.

Vesting:

Contributions to SIMPLE IRAs are immediately 100 percent vested. This means employees own the funds as soon as contributions are made, giving them immediate access to their savings.

Flexibility:

SIMPLE IRAs are easy to set up and administer. Employers can adjust the matching or nonelective contribution percentage annually, within certain limits. However, the chosen contribution method cannot be changed midyear.

Tax-Deferred Growth:

Funds in a SIMPLE IRA grow tax-deferred, meaning taxes on contributions and investment earnings are deferred until withdrawal.

Distributions:

Withdrawals from SIMPLE IRAs are taxed as ordinary income. If funds are withdrawn within the first two years of participation, a 25 percent early withdrawal penalty may apply unless an exception is met. After this period, the standard 10 percent early withdrawal penalty applies for withdrawals before age 59 1/2.

To illustrate how contributions work with a SIMPLE IRA, consider the following scenario: Alex, the owner of a small bakery, has three employees—Lisa, Mark, and Jane. In 2023, Alex implements a 3 percent matching contribution for the SIMPLE IRA plan. Alex's compensation is $80,000, Lisa's is $50,000, Mark's is $35,000, and Jane's is $30,000. Consequently, Alex contributes $2,400 (3 percent of $80,000), Lisa contributes $1,500 (3 percent of $50,000), Mark contributes $1,050 (3 percent of $35,000), and Jane contributes $900 (3 percent of $30,000). In this setup, each employee contributes up to the annual limit or the amount they choose, with Alex matching up to 3 percent of their salaries. These contributions are immediately vested, and both employer and employee contributions offer valuable tax benefits.

Making Sense of the Options

As you can see, there are several retirement plan options tailored to different needs and circumstances. If you are a solopreneur or a small business owner, the SOLO 401(k) offers high contribution limits and the flexibility of choosing between traditional and Roth formats, making it a powerful tool for those with higher incomes and a strong desire to maximize their tax-advantaged savings. SEP IRAs, with their generous contribution limits and straightforward setup, are great for business owners looking to save aggressively while keeping administrative tasks to a minimum. SIMPLE IRAs, on the other hand, provide a more structured approach with required employer contributions, making them ideal for small businesses wanting to encourage employee savings with immediate vesting.

When deciding on the right plan, consider your income, business structure, and the level of administrative complexity you're willing to manage. The right choice will help ensure your retirement savings strategy is as unique as your business.

Part-Time, Seasonal, and Low-Income Workers

The SECURE 2.0 Act has improved access to retirement accounts for part-time and low-income workers. Part-time workers become eligible for employer 401(k) plans after two years of consistent employment. This is significant given the previous requirement was 500 hours per year for three consecutive years.[9] For example, Alex, a part-time retail worker, becomes eligible for his employer's 401(k) plan after two years. He starts contributing 5 percent of his paycheck and takes advantage of his employer's matching contributions.

Importantly, SECURE 2.0 now allows families to offer SEP IRAs to domestic workers like nannies and chefs.[10] For example, Emily, the head of a family with two young children, employs Sarah as a nanny. Sarah has been with

---

9 Taylor, K. R. (2024, June 25). *SECURE 2.0 Act summary: New retirement plan rules to know*. Kiplinger. https://www.kiplinger.com/retirement/secure-20-act-summary-new-retirement-plan-rules-to-know

10 Cohen & Buckmann, P. C. (2023, January 30). *SECURE 2.0 creates new opportunities for IRAs, SEPs, and SIMPLE IRAs*. Cohen & Buckmann, P.C. https://cohenbuckmann.com/secure-2-0-creates-new-opportunities-for-iras-seps-and-simple-iras/

the family for over a year, and Emily wants to offer her a retirement benefit. With SECURE 2.0 in place, Emily can set up a SEP IRA for Sarah. Emily decides to contribute 5 percent of Sarah's salary to the SEP IRA. Sarah earns $40,000 annually, so Emily contributes $2,000 (5 percent of $40,000) to the SEP IRA. This contribution helps Sarah build her retirement savings while providing her with a valuable employee benefit.

Multiple Retirement Accounts

Having multiple types of retirement accounts can maximize your contributions and tax benefits. While you cannot open two of the same accounts (e.g., two Roth IRAs), you can have a 401(k), Roth IRA, and traditional IRA simultaneously. Prioritize contributions to each account type to maximize benefits. For instance, Emma maxes out her contributions to her employer's 401(k) and then opens a Roth IRA. She contributes the maximum allowed to both accounts, taking full advantage of tax benefits and employer matching.

In the multiple-retirement-account scenario, **be mindful of income limits for eligibility to a Roth IRA.**

Other Wealth-Building Accounts

Health Savings Accounts (HSAs) are available to individuals with high-deductible health plans, offering triple-tax benefits. Contributions, growth, and withdrawals for qualified expenses are all tax-free. HSA 2023 contribution limits are $3,850 for self-only coverage and $7,750 for an individual covering their family. Also, taxpayers 55 and older can make an additional $1,000 contribution.

For example, David, who is 48 and covers his family, has a high-deductible health plan. He opens an HSA and contributes $4,150 annually. He invests the funds, and over the years, his HSA grows significantly, providing tax-free money for medical expenses in retirement.

Education savings accounts like 529 plans provide tax-free growth and withdrawals for educational expenses. Unused funds can be rolled over into a dependent's Roth IRA. For instance, Lisa opens a 529 plan for her son's college education. The plan grows tax-free, and if there are leftover funds after her son graduates, she can roll them over into his Roth IRA. As with any transition between accounts, please do your homework to determine eligibility and restrictions.

Prioritizing Investments

Maximize the retirement account that offers you the most significant benefit first, then move to Roth IRAs, traditional IRAs, and other accounts. Taking advantage of employer matches and tax-advantaged accounts is crucial for a robust retirement savings strategy. For example, John contributes to his 401(k) up to the employer match limit, then contributes after tax to a traditional IRA (he earns too much to qualify for a Roth IRA). He starts investing in a traditional IRA with additional funds, even though these contributions are not tax deductible. The benefit to the contributions is the long-term tax-deferred growth on the investments. Finally, when withdrawing his basis (what he originally contributed after tax), he does so tax-free, with growth taxed as ordinary income sometime down the road.

Regardless of how you go about prioritizing your retirement account contributions, **make certain you understand contribution limits, income limits, and tax implications when making contributions as well as when taking distributions.**

Conclusion

As we've explored, there are numerous retirement account options beyond the traditional 401(k), each tailored to different financial situations and employment statuses. From IRAs and HSAs to specialized plans for freelancers and business owners, these alternatives provide flexibility and valuable tax benefits. Whether you're a solopreneur, a part-time worker, or an individual without access to an employer-sponsored plan, it's crucial to understand and leverage these opportunities to secure your financial future.

By thoughtfully prioritizing your investments and staying informed about the latest regulations and benefits, such as those introduced by the SECURE 2.0 Act, you can build a robust and diversified retirement portfolio. Remember, a well-planned retirement strategy is not just about saving money but also about making informed decisions that align with your long-term goals. So take charge of your financial destiny, and don't hesitate to seek professional advice to navigate the complexities of retirement planning.

Key Points from Chapter 8

1. **Alternatives for Those without a 401(k):** There are many retirement account options besides the

traditional 401(k) for those who do not have access to one at work, including IRAs, SOLO 401(k)s SIMPLE IRAs, and SEP IRAs.

2. **Individual Retirement Accounts (IRAs):** Traditional IRAs offer tax deductions on contributions and tax-free growth until retirement, while Roth IRAs provide tax-free growth and withdrawals since contributions are made with after-tax income.

3. **Options for the Self-Employed and Business Owners:** SOLO 401(k)s allow for substantial contributions (up to $66,000 in 2023) and can be structured as traditional or Roth accounts. SEP IRAs and SIMPLE IRAs offer flexible and advantageous retirement savings options for small business owners and their employees.

4. **Part-Time, Seasonal, and Low-Income Workers:** The SECURE 2.0 Act has improved access to retirement accounts for part-time workers, domestic workers, and low-income earners, allowing them to benefit from retirement savings incentives.

5. **Multiple Retirement Accounts:** You can open multiple types of retirement accounts (e.g., 401(k), Roth IRA, traditional IRA) to maximize contributions and tax benefits, providing flexibility in your retirement savings strategy.

6. **Other Wealth-Building Accounts:** Health Savings Accounts (HSAs) offer triple-tax benefits for those with high-deductible health plans. Education savings accounts like 529 plans provide tax advantages for saving for educational expenses and can be rolled over into a dependent's Roth IRA if unused.

7. **Strategic Investment Prioritization:** Prioritize contributions to 401(k) accounts, followed by Roth IRAs, traditional IRAs, and then other investment options. Maximizing employer matches and tax-advantaged accounts is key to a robust retirement savings strategy.

CHAPTER 9

FINANCIAL INDEPENDENCE, RETIRE EARLY (FIRE): A RADICAL APPROACH

The millennial generation has given us a number of financial game-changers. I'm talking about things like Bitcoin and Ethereum (hello, crypto millionaires!), robo-advisors, and DIY investment apps like Betterment and Robinhood. And let's not forget mobile payment tech like Venmo and Apple Pay—because who carries cash anymore? Oh, and we can't skip the meme stock revolution led by the one and only Keith Gill, aka "Roaring Kitty" and "DeepF***ingValue." Can a group of retail investors actually bring a multibillion-dollar hedge fund to its knees (hello, Melvin)?

But here's the real gem from millennials: the FIRE movement—Financial Independence, Retire Early. Yep, it's the dream of living your best life without waiting until you're 65. Go millennials! Throughout this book, we've suggested that you save between 10 and 15 percent of your take-home pay to invest in retirement. However, supporters of the FIRE movement might find this amusingly conservative. If you struggle to save that 10 to 15 percent, you might want to skip to the next section. But read on if you're intrigued by the philosophy of saving aggressively now to gain financial freedom sooner.

The Philosophy of FIRE

The FIRE movement fundamentally opposes the traditional work-life span of 20 to 60 years. Having gained traction among millennials in the 2010s through online media platforms, podcasts, and videos, FIRE has as its core objective achieving financial independence and retiring early by living off passive income. This is typically guided by the 4% Rule, which suggests that one can sustainably withdraw 4 percent of their investment portfolio annually to cover living expenses. This means that to live the "FIRE way," one must save and invest 25 times their average annual expenses to never have to work again. Naturally, such a radical approach has its critics, but there are valuable lessons to be learned from the FIRE adherents.

The Roots of FIRE

The FIRE movement is rooted in the book *Your Money or Your Life*.[11] The movement underscores the importance

---

11 Robin, V., & Dominguez, J. (2008). *Your money or your life: 9 steps to transforming your relationship with money and achieving financial independence: Fully revised and updated for 2018.* Penguin.

of changing your relationship with your money to achieve financial freedom. At the heart of the FIRE movement is the challenge to cut expenses to the bare minimum. While there is no single leader of this movement, some more vocal advocates suggest saving 50 percent of one's income, with extreme proponents even advocating for saving a staggering 75 percent.

The movement encourages individuals to find ways to boost their income and invest more in the stock market. One of the key strategies is to maximize contributions to retirement accounts to reduce taxable income. Many books, articles, and media productions emphasize investing in a 401(k) as a primary step. The FIRE approach demands consistent saving and investing behavior, alongside significant sacrifices for many. Consequently, FIRE is often viewed as a lifestyle rather than a financial strategy.

Insights from Research

Researchers Khan and Pandey took a deep dive into the fascinating world of FIRE. In their study, rooted in netnography (a quantitative research method focused on studying online communities and cultures) and published in the *Journal of Consumer Marketing*, the authors highlight the movement's focus on aggressive savings and smart investments to achieve early retirement. The authors uncover the driving forces, behaviors, and communal bonds that define the FIRE community by examining lively discussions and rich exchanges in forums and social media. Key themes like frugality, savvy investment tactics, and the supportive role of online networks come to light.[12]

Key Tenets of FIRE

How does this relate to the advice in this book? Most individuals who have achieved financial independence, through any means, adhere to the practices we advocate for in this book. At the same time, it is supported by quantitative research of online FIRE communities. A short list of FIRE tenets includes:

- Maximizing 401(k) deferrals

- Capturing the full company match

- Investing in low-cost index-focused equity investments

- Eliminating debt

- Creating and sticking to a budget

- Saving and investing at least 10 to 15 percent of income

In short, the tenets of the FIRE movement complement our advice but are more extreme. Followers of FIRE are not

---

12 Khan, A. W., & Pandey, J. (2023). Exploring fire for financial independence retire early (FIRE): A netnography approach. *Journal of Consumer Marketing*, *40*(6), 775–784.

wrong; they are just different. If you choose to pursue this path, understand that it's a significant lifestyle change and not something we recommend for everyone. You can still enjoy a good life and a fulfilling retirement by following the steps outlined in this book. Remember, this is not a race or a game; this is your life.

Diving Deeper into FIRE

Let's delve deeper into its core principles and practices to grasp the FIRE movement fully. Beyond its emphasis on aggressive saving, investing, and the 4% Rule, the FIRE movement includes the following key tenets:

Cutting Expenses

FIRE followers are known for their frugality. This might mean living in a smaller home, driving an older car, or forgoing expensive vacations. The idea is to cut expenses to the bone, allowing for maximum savings and investment. This extreme frugality is often a point of contention and criticism, but the payoff is worth the sacrifice for those who adopt it.

Increasing Income

While cutting expenses is one side of the coin, increasing income is the other. FIRE advocates often seek side hustles, freelance work, or high-paying careers to boost their income. The goal is to accelerate the path to financial independence by maximizing the money available for investment.

Tax Efficiency
Minimizing taxes is a critical strategy for FIRE enthusiasts. This involves taking full advantage of tax-advantaged accounts like 401(k)s, IRAs, and HSAs. By lowering taxable income and maximizing investment growth, FIRE followers can reach their goals more quickly.

Variations within the FIRE Movement

There are several iterations within the FIRE movement, each tailored to different levels of frugality and income:

1. **Fat FIRE:** This approach is for those who aim for financial independence without significantly sacrificing their current standard of living. It requires a higher income to sustain savings and investments at the desired level.

2. **Lean FIRE:** This approach emphasizes extreme frugality, allowing individuals to retire early with minimal living expenses. Lean FIRE followers often live on very modest budgets both before and after retirement.

3. **Barista FIRE:** A hybrid approach where individuals achieve partial financial independence, allowing them to work part-time jobs (such as being a barista) to cover some expenses while their investments cover the rest. This strategy provides a balance between work and leisure.

Criticism of FIRE

Despite its popularity, the FIRE movement is not without its critics. Some argue that it promotes an unrealistic and overly frugal lifestyle that sacrifices too much for the sake of early retirement. Others point out that it relies heavily on the assumption of continued market growth, which may not always be the case.

Conclusion

While the extreme measures of the FIRE movement are not for everyone, its principles can still offer valuable lessons. Even if saving 75 percent of your income is unrealistic, aiming to increase your savings rate beyond the traditional 10 to 15 percent can significantly impact your financial future. Balancing FIRE's aggressive saving and investing strategies with a sustainable and enjoyable lifestyle is key.

As significantly, the FIRE movement represents a radical shift in how we think about work, savings, and retirement. By challenging traditional norms and advocating for extreme saving and investing, FIRE offers a path to financial independence that can be both inspiring and daunting. Whether you choose to fully embrace the FIRE lifestyle or incorporate some of its principles into your financial plan, the ultimate goal remains the same: achieving financial freedom and living life on your terms.

Remember, this journey is personal and unique to each individual. It's not about comparing yourself to others but finding the best balance for you. This is your life; your financial strategy should reflect your values, goals, and aspirations.

Key Points from Chapter 9

1. **Origins and Popularity:** The FIRE movement, rooted in the book *Your Money or Your Life,* by Vicki Robin and Joe Dominguez (2008), gained popularity among millennials in the 2010s through online platforms, podcasts, and videos. It challenges the traditional work-life span of 20 to 60 years by advocating for aggressive saving and investing to achieve financial independence and early retirement.

2. **The 4% Rule:** Central to the FIRE philosophy is the 4% Rule, which suggests that withdrawing 4 percent of your investment portfolio annually can sustainably cover living expenses in retirement. This requires saving and investing 25 times your annual expenses.

3. **Aggressive Saving and Investing:** FIRE advocates push for saving upward of 50 to 75 percent of income, significantly more than the traditional financial advice of 10 to 15 percent. This involves a radical rethinking of spending habits and lifestyle choices, prioritizing long-term freedom over short-term comforts.

4. **Frugality and Increasing Income:** Followers of FIRE are known for their extreme frugality, cutting expenses to the bare minimum. They also seek

ways to boost their income through side hustles, freelance work, or high-paying careers to maximize investments.

5. **Tax Efficiency:** Minimizing taxes is crucial for FIRE enthusiasts. This includes leveraging tax-advantaged accounts like 401(k)s, IRAs, and HSAs to lower taxable income and maximize investment growth.

6. **Flexibility Within FIRE**: While the FIRE movement is often seen as extreme, it's far from monolithic. Different approaches within FIRE—ranging from more conservative strategies that allow for a comfortable lifestyle to minimalist approaches that prioritize frugality—demonstrate that there's flexibility in how individuals can pursue financial independence.

7. **Criticism and Balance:** Critics argue that FIRE promotes an unrealistic, overly frugal lifestyle and relies heavily on market growth assumptions. However, balancing FIRE's aggressive strategies with a sustainable lifestyle can still offer valuable financial lessons.

CHAPTER 10

THE LATE BLOOMERS: IT'S NEVER TOO LATE TO START SAVING

Do you feel like you missed the boat on saving for retirement? Think again! There's plenty you can do right now to boost your financial future, no matter your age. Imagine you're 60 and your retirement savings account looks a bit bare. Maybe you were busy helping your kids through college, taking care of a sick parent, or spoiling your grandkids. Don't sweat it! There's still hope. You might wish you'd started saving in your 401(k) earlier, but hey, you were investing in your loved ones, so give yourself a break. But delay no more!

Meet Steve: The Ultimate Giver

Years ago, I met a guy named Steve, a true giver. Steve had taken care of everyone except himself, figuring he'd work forever (which, if you remember from previous chapters, could be your plan A versus plan B). He and his wife lived simply on one income, paid off their debts and most of their mortgage, and put three kids through college but had little left for retirement. I told Steve it wasn't too late to save but it would require some sacrifices. To make it work, they'd need to focus on retirement and keep working until 70. This would maximize their 401(k) contributions, snag employer matching funds, and boost their Social Security benefits by retiring after the full retirement age.

Steve's Turnaround Plan
At 60, with only $50,000 saved for retirement, Steve took my advice. He upped his 401(k) contributions from his $72,000 salary to 10 percent, took advantage of his employer's 4 percent match, and invested in a balanced account with an expected 8 percent return. By working an additional 10 years, Steve's retirement account was estimated to grow to around $275,000, with Social Security benefits of about $2,000 per month instead of $1,700 if he retired at 65. Steve discovered he still had a lot to offer his company and found joy in continuing to work, knowing he was securing the future he wanted.

Living the Dream
By 2018 Steve and his wife were living on about $3,600 a month. If they retired in 2023, they'd need roughly $4,200, depending on where they decided to settle down. With $2,000 from Social Security and $1,600 from retirement savings, they were able to cover all their needs and then some, without debt. Steve was thrilled he didn't give up

on retirement but instead made a final push for savings in his last working years. His story shows that with wisdom, support, and action, it's never too late to retire well.

Your Turn: Make the Most of Now

So if you're feeling like you've missed your chance, take heart. Whether you're 20, 40, or 60, there's always something you can do to improve your financial future. Start saving, keep investing, and remember—it's never too late to build the retirement of your dreams.

Late Bloomer Tips

First, refer to chapter 2, where I summarized the SECURE 2.0. For this chapter's topic, we can just focus on the two big takeaways for those 50 and older:

1. **Catch-up contributions have increased** from $6,500 to $7,500 in retirement accounts.

2. **By 2025, people aged 60 to 63 will be able to add up to $10,000** in catch-up contributions.

Have you ever heard the Chinese proverb "The best time to plant a tree is twenty years ago. The second-best time is now"? I'm not saying this is going to be easy if you were late to the saving and investing game. It will take some effort, but it can be done!

An important task you will need to complete before retiring is to evaluate your timeline. Be realistic here. How long can you actually work before retiring? Some people may have to work into their 70s—and there is nothing wrong with that. There are many people who are well-off but they continue to work as long their work is rewarding.

If you are a late bloomer, you should consider hiring a financial advisor to go over your financial plan. They can guide you through the work-to-retirement transition and show you a realistic look at your situation. Not to mention, they can help you pick investments that fit your goal as well as offer advice on taxes and many other services.

Retiring later than you expected can be a bummer, but it's not the end of the world. You can still find rewarding work and help secure the rest of your life. There are many prominent examples of people who achieved financial success later in their lives:

- **Pablo Picasso** accumulated most of his wealth late in his life and even after he died!

- **Judge Judy** did not start her TV program until she was 54.

- **Warren Buffett** (Remember him?) is worth north of $100 billion—most of which was accumulated after normal retirement age.

I hope you understand that you can still have a good life whether you are retired at a certain point or not. Even if you still need to work, understand that the work can still be rewarding for yourself, your organization, your community, and the greater country.

Embracing the Journey Ahead

As we close this chapter, remember that it's never too late to take control of your financial future. Whether you're starting late or refining your strategy, the key is to take action now. With thoughtful planning, the right support, and a commitment to your goals, you can achieve the retirement you desire. So plant that tree today, nurture it with care, and watch your financial future grow strong and resilient. Your best days of financial security and peace of mind are still ahead.

Key Points from Chapter 10

1. **It's Never Too Late to Start Saving:** Even if you begin saving for retirement at 60, you can still make significant improvements to your financial situation. It's important to focus on what you can do now rather than lamenting missed opportunities in the past.

2. **Maximizing Contributions and Benefits:** Increasing contributions to your retirement accounts, taking advantage of employer matching, and working until 70 can substantially boost your retirement savings and Social Security benefits.

3. **Strategic Financial Planning:** Hiring a financial advisor can be crucial, especially for late bloomers. Advisors can help you create a realistic plan,

select appropriate investments, and navigate the transition from working to retirement.

4. **Understanding Catch-Up Contributions:** The SECURE 2.0 allows increased catch-up contributions for those aged 50 and older. By 2025, individuals aged 60 to 63 will be able to contribute an additional $10,000, providing a significant boost to retirement savings.

5. **Creating a Safe Bucket:** Maintaining three to five years' worth of cash on hand in a "safe bucket" can provide stability and reduce anxiety about market volatility, ensuring you have funds readily available for immediate needs.

6. **Evaluating Your Timeline:** Realistically assessing how long you can work before retiring is essential. Many individuals may need to work into their 70s, which can still be rewarding and provide additional financial security.

7. **Inspiration from Late Bloomers:** Numerous successful individuals, such as Pablo Picasso and Judge Judy, achieved significant financial success later in life. Their stories demonstrate that it's possible to find fulfillment and financial stability at any age.

CHAPTER 11

INSPIRING SAVERS: REAL STORIES OF HOPE

I have learned that sharing real stories of retirement helps to create hope in our financial future. So my hope is that telling you about real-world retirement planners like Lula, John, Maria, David, and Ruth allows me to bring to light that saving and investing through retirement accounts like a 401(k) is both possible and wise. It's true, taking the time to learn the basics about the 401(k) and retirement takes some effort—as does foregoing a portion of your paycheck today so you can live comfortably in the future. But my intention with this book is to show you that the effort pays off manyfold in your retirement (or refirement) years, whatever they might look like.

Sometimes, we look at people who seem to be riding the wave of financial success and wonder, "What is their secret?" Well, I'm here to tell you there is no secret—just a little knowledge, an employer that values you and your financial well-being, and some financial discipline on your part.

It reminds me a bit of the scene in *Kung Fu Panda* where Po and Master Shifu are at the Jade Palace, standing before the ancient and revered Dragon Scroll, which is believed to hold the ultimate secret to limitless power and becoming the true Dragon Warrior. Po is filled with anticipation and excitement as he finally has the scroll. Po carefully unrolls the scroll, expecting to find profound wisdom and a powerful secret, only to realize it is blank. But as he looks deeper into the scroll's reflective surface, he understands that the secret is him. In other words, retirement success can, in large part, be dictated by you.

Worse than believing there is some secret to retirement saving success is believing there is a fast and easy way to it. "Fast" and "retirement success" are not two words I would want you to believe should go together. Despite what you might see on TV, hear from your neighbor, or glean from your favorite social media personality, there is no secret and there is no fast way to it.

If you can come to terms with the fact that earning money and saving for retirement takes (1) a little discipline and awareness and (2) time, you will be on your way to success! Even small investments for those of you making $15 an hour can mean retiring with $1 million at retirement age, if you stay employed and save. The wealthy become wealthier through how they approach their investments once they start saving, and you can take the same approach. Whatever your financial stripes, they can change over a lifetime, given this not-so-secret knowledge of what to do with your savings once you start to save.

The Importance of Wealth Building

Why is wealth building so important? Having a wealth-building mindset is sometimes misconstrued as greed. But in fact wealth building is the intentional focus on how you make and save money. It can help you achieve financial freedom, change your family financial tree, build generational wealth, start a business, take on philanthropic pursuits, and much more. A foundational aspect of wealth building is a 401(k) or similar retirement account, which allows you to save and invest over a long period systematically.

There is no secret to how many of our very wealthiest clients have accumulated their wealth. First, they find work or create a job for themselves. Once working, they prioritize saving and investing. For most of us, this is possible too. While it is not complex, you must pay attention. Unfortunately, as previously shared, there is no surefire way to accumulate assets quickly. I have yet to hear of a get-rich-quick scheme that didn't either fail miserably or land the "smart guys" in jail.

Getting a job and staying employed while saving and investing over a lifetime is the best game plan for today, tomorrow, and every day after. Wealth takes time to grow. Retirement investing is not a get-rich-quick scheme. Do you remember Warren, Maria, and Ruth? They understood there is no secret to creating retirement wealth, nor is there a quick way there.

The Path to Wealth

Most of the wealthy individuals I have met did not start rich. They bought cars known for their endurance, not their looks, and drove them as long as possible. They bought a house and kept it, and then bought another house and kept that, and then bought yet another, and so on. They didn't sell their first homes so they could get bigger ones. They applied a little discipline to budgeting and saving while learning along the way. And one day, not so suddenly, they had a lot.

There is a false belief in America that many wealthy people inherited their wealth. This is not true. And more to the point, thinking that many individuals and families have inherited their wealth emphasizes waiting for a handout from the family instead of controlling what you can achieve on your own.

Savings guru Dave Ramsey conducted meaningful research on inherited wealth. He and his team published a sweeping millionaire study and found 79 percent of millionaires were self-made. The same report noted that just 2 percent of millionaires came from "upper-income" households. The study also stated that only a few of the other 21 percent who received an inheritance received $100,000 or more. Finally, and importantly, eight in ten millionaires surveyed reported investing in their 401(k) plan.[13] This statistic on millionaires and their savings rate in their 401(k) is

---

13 Ramsey Solutions. (2024, June 11). *The National Study of Millionaires: The American dream is alive and available*. https://www.ramseysolutions.com/retirement/the-national-study-of-millionaires-research

in stark contrast to a 2022 government report highlighting that just 35 percent of individuals surveyed had a 401(k) plan.[14] The connection between 401(k) participation and building meaningful wealth is clear: small amounts invested well over a long time offers most American workers the opportunity to retire a millionaire too.

Overcoming Humble Beginnings

Surprisingly, a disproportionate number of people I have worked with grew up in financially humble circumstances. I find it interesting that the wealthy are viewed as being given what they have when, in fact, the numbers tell a different story. In a recent study, Bank of America surveyed over 1,000 wealthy customers. Nearly 70 percent of wealthy respondents reported not receiving any inheritance. Also, 25 percent of respondents self-identified as having a poor or middle-class upbringing—reinforcing my view that wealth is earned, not inherited.[15]

For me and those reading along, knowing that the rich were not always rich means there is hope for all of us. Fortunes are built, not bestowed. If we can follow the saving and investing habits of the wealthy, we can potentially have a more secure retirement lifestyle without depending on an inheritance to us get there.

---

14 U.S. Census Bureau. (2022, August 2). *Who has retirement accounts?* https://www.census.gov/library/stories/2022/08/who-has-retirement-accounts.html

15 Bank of America Private Bank. (2024). *2024 Bank of America Private Bank Study of Wealthy Americans*. https://www.private-bank.bankofamerica.com/articles/generational-divide-wealth-study.html

In addition to their humble beginnings, many of the wealthy treat their investments differently than your average investor. The same Bank of America survey notes that once wealthy investors own an investment, they hold on to it, letting it accumulate over time instead of selling it. They view their investments more as heirlooms to be held and cared for than sports cards or horses that are traded. This is particularly true for those aged 21 to 43, who tend to favor long-term strategies while consistently investing over time.

I don't necessarily subscribe to a buy-and-hold mentality. What I do recommend is buying consistently over a long time and assessing your portfolio on an ongoing basis, whether it's in your 401(k) or outside of it. You'll find that if you are committed to buying over a lifetime and purchasing investments with a strong track record of performance, then you'll likely end up holding those same investments forever.

Investing for the Long Haul

When it comes to 401(k) investing, we see far too many employees checking their investments daily and investing based on emotion rather than a plan. This is a bad idea for many reasons, the most important being that the odds of success are slim to none. The way to be financially secure and independent is to invest in your 401(k) savings regularly over a long time and direct as many dollars as possible into an appropriately diversified, low-cost investment. That's it. Investing and monitoring over time is the best approach and the one we've seen our most financially successful clients use, both in and out of retirement plans.

With real estate, the game plan is similar, although done primarily outside of a 401(k) plan. I saw clients Sherry and William do this when they drew closer to retirement. They had accumulated commercial buildings, residential property, and various other assets. As they went along, they were not looking to add to their portfolio but to upgrade it and find gaps in their investing. They bought and held many of their homes for a lifetime (after more than 60 years of ownership, the family recently sold the home the kids were raised in). Also, they were unafraid to take an asset they had owned for only five years and roll it into another to upgrade their investment portfolio.

The key to their success was being good savers and consistent investors, and constantly monitoring what they had to see if it met their needs. There were years when the gains were small or there may have been some loss, but that did not cause them to sell everything or get discouraged. This stability paid off. They did very well over their lifetime.

The Common Approach to Wealth Building

It's the same with the stock market. It is common to see a client accumulate a portfolio of stocks and upgrade it occasionally throughout the year. If an investor owns shares in 60 companies, buying and holding means maintaining a core of 40 to 50 companies each year while swapping out one investment for another to upgrade the portfolio.

Other investors may have massive gains in a company they founded, were an executive of, or were employed at for a long time. We have seen this with our friends and neighbors, Intel and Nike employees. They have worked for the same company for a long time, accumulating the company's stock. When they sell, they often reinvest to upgrade their portfolios with diversified companies, such as those in real estate, timber, and cryptocurrency. The upgrade is not about owning a better company; Nike and Intel have been good investments over the years. Instead, it is about selling to lock in the gains (growth of the investment) while reducing the risk of owning just one company's stock. Again, it is all about saving, investing, accumulating, and monitoring those assets over a lifetime while making shifts to upgrade the portfolio when necessary.

The commonality among these financially secure individuals is that they worked hard and understood that they needed to save—oftentimes leveraging their 401(k) and other retirement savings vehicles. Whether by accident or intentionally, they didn't make a habit of buying and selling but rather bought and held. They made a habit of being lifetime investors and accumulators of good investments.

Unfortunately, this simple but highly effective method for becoming wealthy is not sexy and will not win you an audience at a cocktail party. But here's the great news: it works, and it can be used by the rich and those of us with more humble circumstances. Remember, most wealthy individuals and their families did not start out rich; instead, they used the methods of the rich to accumulate wealth over time.

Avoiding the Temptation of Get-Rich-Quick Schemes

Taking such a patient approach to wealth building is not necessarily easy—as I've learned through decades of experience with clients. Too many individuals are drawn to the ego-driven, adrenaline-rush, challenge-inducing world of beating the market. In the investing world, "trying to beat the market" means attempting to achieve investment returns that are higher than the stock market's average returns, typically represented by a market index like the S&P 500. Investors who try to beat the market often engage in active trading, selecting individual stocks or other investments they believe will outperform the overall market.

This is an ill-advised strategy, especially when it comes to your 401(k) retirement assets. Very few people can consistently beat the market, and that is why I'm so bullish on investing in low-cost index mutual funds and exchange-traded funds (ETFs).

For your reference, I've included a chart from the S&P Index Verus Active report (SPIVA) highlighting the challenges of trying to get rich quickly by "beating" the market. For instance, over 10 years, 87.42 percent of all large-cap US equity funds underperformed the S&P 500. So with low odds of outpacing the market through active trading and other get-rich-quick schemes, I suggest investing in low-cost index funds—particularly when investing in your 401(k). This is the route I've taken to becoming a 401(k) millionaire.

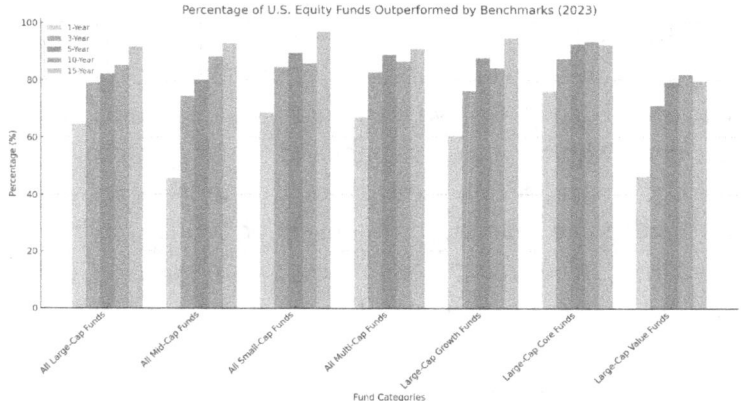

SPIVA US Year-End 2023 Report

Real-Life Examples of Wealth Building

A good friend and client of mine, Dan, went to school on the East Coast, started working in the beverage industry, and later became an executive at a publicly traded company. He negotiated for as much stock in the company as possible (in lieu of a bigger salary) and piled a ton of his capital into his 401(k) and deferred compensation plan. Dan was able to refire (fire himself from working day-to-day and ignite his fire for consulting and golf) in his early 50s.

Dan has been working, saving, and investing since he was a kid—his story is certainly not one of overnight success. Now that he's accumulated retirement wealth, he's made never having to go back to work all but certain through a disciplined approach to spending. New cars for Dan? Nope. First class flying—never. Country club—that's funny. Generous? Very. He and his wife live an amazing life because they took a small portion of his paycheck and deferred it into a 401(k) with a matching employer contribution for 20-plus years.

Or take Julie and Raymond, two wonderful clients of our firm. Julie and Ray married young, started a family, and for the most part made humble salaries their whole lives. In the mid-1970s they bought their first home in Portland, Oregon, and lived in it for many years before it was worth just a little more than what they paid for it. When it was time to sell their home, they rolled the proceeds into another home. This was not a big money-making decision; they needed more room as their family grew. Over time, as their incomes started to rise and real estate started to do very well, they kept the homes they lived in and accumulated one after another.

Rarely did they buy a new car. In fact, they often purchased a nicely depreciated used car. They did not focus on lifestyle spending; they understood that if they focused on living, working, and saving, it would pay off in the end, and it did! As Dave Ramsey says, "Live like no one else now, so you can live, and give, like no one else later."

Julie and Raymond have helped countless families, nonprofits, their church, and many, many neighbors, all because they have been big on working, saving, and investing in their retirement accounts and small on spending for decades. For some, being a good saver may mean a bigger, more financially luxurious life at or during retirement. For others, the ability to share the benefits of a life well lived is what financial discipline can afford. Whatever your bent is, it starts with having a job and saving and investing over a lifetime.

Conclusion

As you reflect on these stories, as well as those of Lula, John, Maria, David, and Ruth, remember that the path to financial security and a comfortable retirement isn't hidden in some secret formula or quick-fix scheme. It's a journey paved with disciplined saving, consistent investing, and a long-term perspective.

These real-life examples demonstrate that with patience, dedication, and the right approach, anyone can build a robust financial future. Whether you're just starting out or well on your way, keep in mind that the power to secure your retirement lies within you. Embrace the knowledge, leverage the tools available, and commit to the process. The wealth you seek is not beyond your reach; it's a reflection of your efforts and smart choices. So take that first step, stay the course, and look forward to the financial freedom that awaits you.

Key Points from the Chapter 11

1. **Real Stories of Success:** Examples, like those of Lula, John, and others, prove that anyone—regardless of their financial starting point—can achieve a secure retirement with steady, disciplined savings.

2. **The Power of Consistent Saving:** Consistent saving is paramount, and it has a major impact on your

long-term financial security. Small, regular contributions can grow significantly over time.

3. **No Secret to Success:** Financial success involves understanding the basics, having a supportive employer, and practicing financial discipline.

4. **Avoiding Get-Rich-Quick Schemes:** Many pitfalls exist when trying to make a quick buck. Understand that financial stability comes from long-term planning and disciplined investing, not from risky, short-term strategies.

5. **Wealth Building through 401(k) Plans:** 401(k) plans and other retirement accounts play a crucial role in building wealth systematically over time. Most millionaires have leveraged these tools effectively.

6. **The Importance of a Wealth-Building Mindset:** Building a mindset focused on making and saving money intentionally can lead to financial freedom, generational wealth, and the ability to pursue philanthropic goals.

7. **Learning from Real-Life Examples:** Dan, Julie, Raymond, Sherry, and William illustrate practical ways of saving, investing, and managing finances. Their disciplined approaches to saving, avoiding unnecessary expenses, and upgrading

investments can serve as models for you and your saving journey.

PART III: TO RETIRE IS HUMAN

CHAPTER 12

MARKET TIMING, THE NEWS, AND YOUR EMOTIONS

Up to this point, we've covered the nuts and bolts of retirement savings accounts, stressed the magic of starting early and saving consistently, and explored the many perks of investing in a 401(k). Now, we will switch gears and begin to examine the importance of discipline, systematic investment approaches like dollar-cost averaging, and the role of emotion and behavior in investing success.

When it comes to investing, discipline is a must. The best-laid plans can unravel if you let your emotions take the wheel. It is like driving with your eyes closed—it's bound to end in disaster. Take, for example, the investor who panics during a market downturn and sells off all their assets at rock-bottom prices, locking in losses instead of riding out the storm. Or the one who chases the latest "hot stock" because of fear of missing out, only to watch it plummet soon after jumping in. These knee-jerk reactions are common pitfalls that can derail even the most promising financial plans.

On the flip side, having a steady hand—like that of the investor who sticks to their strategy through thick and thin—can pay off big-time. By staying calm, ignoring the noise, and keeping their eyes on the long-term prize, these investors often emerge from market dips with their portfolios intact and their gains compounding. It's the difference between being a leaf tossed around by the wind and a tree that stands firm, growing stronger through every season.

So how do you keep your cool when the market is playing tricks on your nerves? The key lies in using strategies that take emotion out of the equation and put your investments on autopilot. One of the most effective ways to do this is through dollar-cost averaging. This strategy isn't about trying to outsmart the market or timing your investments perfectly; instead, it's about embracing consistency and routine, investing a fixed amount regularly, whether the market is soaring or sinking. By sticking to this disciplined approach, you sidestep the temptation to make rash decisions based on fear or greed, allowing you to stay the course even when emotions run high. Let's explore how dollar-cost averaging can be your secret weapon for steady, reliable investing.

Dollar-Cost Averaging: The Steady Eddy Approach

Dollar-cost averaging is an investment approach where the investor buys a particular investment or group of investments with a set dollar amount on a regular schedule. For example, a 401(k) participant might contribute $100 a month to her account, and those dollars buy her preselected funds on an ongoing basis. The greatest benefit of this approach is that investors don't have to think about buying at a certain price. The automation of dollar-cost averaging allows investors to buy regularly whether the price is up or down. Sometimes an investor is able to buy more shares, sometimes fewer, but when she averages her monthly purchases, she often pays less than the market price for the investment.

A Tale of Five Investors

Charles Schwab's research piece "Does Market Timing Work?"[16] beautifully illustrates the futility of market timing. The study considers five investors: Peter Perfect, Ashley Action, Matthew Monthly, Rosie Rotten, and Larry Linger.

- **Peter Perfect** was an ideal market timer and had the incredible good fortune of buying at the market low each month.

- **Ashley Action** took the most consistent approach, investing her money as soon as it was available.

- **Matthew Monthly**, my personal hero, divided his estimated annual investment by 12, similar to how

---

16 Riepe, M. W. (2013, December 16). *Does market timing work?* Charles Schwab.

many of us invest in our retirement accounts, with a little taken out of each paycheck.

- **Rosie Rotten** had terrible market timing, investing at the market's peak each year.

- **Larry Linger**, Mr. Ultraconservative, kept his money in cash out of fear or neglect.

Surprisingly, even Rosie didn't have the worst outcome; Larry did. The reality is that over the last 100 years, the odds of earning money in the stock market in any calendar year have been more than 70 percent. So naturally, if someone invests their money in the market, regardless of timing, they are likely to earn more than someone who keeps their money in cash.

The Temptation of Market Timing

Market timing is tempting, especially when news headlines scream doom and gloom. But even during events like COVID-19, the Russian invasion of Ukraine, and the chaos of the 2020 US presidential election, the stock markets often defy expectations. For instance, the US stock market rallied more than 5 percent after the Brexit vote and the US election, outperforming cautious investors who stayed in cash.

Even when the market is down—as we saw from 1962 to 1981—investors who dollar-cost average benefit. Only perfect timing or staying in cash the entire time resulted in better returns, but remember, 20 years is just a fraction of an investor's lifetime. This is why Vanguard keeps a portion of all its target retirement funds in stocks, understanding that over a lifetime, keeping money in stocks pays off more than 70 percent of the time.

This is all to say, perfect timing is a myth. If you can consistently pick the perfect time to invest, I'd recommend doing so, but evidence suggests that's nearly impossible. For short periods, someone who does this might look like a genius, but over time, consistently investing in the stock market is the best choice for most retirement investors. It's the consistency of contributions and the length of time invested that pays off, not trying to time the market.

Hidden Costs of Market Timing

Trying to time the market can also be costly. Short-term trading fees, capital gains taxes, and other charges can erode your returns. These fees are designed to protect funds from big in-and-out flows and to discourage unhealthy investing habits. Be aware of these costs and understand how they impact your 401(k) accounts.

Embrace Consistency over Control

Market timers attempt to control the uncontrollable, often driven by fear. Predicting the market's direction is impossible, and emotions are the worst guide for making investment decisions. For every market timer who boasts of a winning trade, there are many more who've been wrong time and again.

If you're a market timer or speculator, consider shifting your strategy. Bet on the global economy's long-term growth with a diversified portfolio of low-cost equity index funds. The odds are in your favor, especially as you invest consistently over time.

Why Dollar-Cost Averaging Works

Loss aversion theory suggests that losses are felt more acutely than gains, making market volatility a significant emotional challenge. Dollar-cost averaging helps mitigate this by spreading out investments and reducing the impact of market fluctuations. It keeps you investing steadily, avoiding the pitfalls of trying to predict the market's next move.

For those unfazed by market turbulence, putting all your money to work immediately can optimize returns. But for most, the emotional roller coaster is too much to bear, leading to panic selling and missed opportunities. Dollar-cost averaging, the reason behind much of the 401(k) investor's success, offers a balanced, less stressful approach.

Wrapping Up: The Power of Consistent Investing

In conclusion, while market timing might seem tempting, it's a strategy fraught with pitfalls and stress. Dollar-cost averaging offers a more reliable, less stressful approach to investing, helping you build wealth steadily over time. Stay the course, ignore the noise, and let the power of consistent investing work for you. In the next chapter, we'll dive deeper into the role of emotions in investing and how to manage them for long-term success.

Key Points from Chapter 12

1. **Avoid Market Timing:** Trying to predict the market's highs and lows is nearly impossible and often leads to poor investment decisions. Instead of chasing the perfect moment, focus on consistent investing.

2. **Embrace Dollar-Cost Averaging:** This simple strategy of investing a fixed amount at regular intervals helps you avoid the pitfalls of market timing, smooths out market volatility, and keeps your investment plan on track.

3. **Consistency is Key:** Consistent investing, no matter the market conditions, is one of the most reliable ways to build wealth over time. It's not about timing the market but spending time in the market.

4. **Stay the Course:** Emotional decisions, like panic selling during downturns or jumping on hot stocks, can derail your financial plans. A steady, disciplined approach to investing helps you navigate through market ups and downs.

5. **Long-Term Focus:** Keeping a long-term perspective allows you to ride out short-term market fluctuations and benefit from the market's general upward trend over time. Remember, investing is a marathon, not a sprint.

6. **Diversification Matters:** Spread your investments across a mix of assets to reduce risk. A diversified portfolio can help balance the ups and downs of the market, providing more stability to your investment journey.

7. **Embrace the Boring:** The best investing strategies aren't flashy or exciting—they're consistent and methodical. Tools like dollar-cost averaging and buy-and-hold investing are simple, effective, and free ways to achieve financial success.

CHAPTER 13

MASTERING THE MIND: NAVIGATING INVESTOR BEHAVIOR AND EMOTIONS

In the previous chapter, we explored the critical role of discipline, maintaining a long-term focus, and leveraging tools like dollar-cost averaging. These strategies aren't just about numbers—they're about steering your behavior in the right direction. At their core, these approaches are designed to help investors concentrate on what truly matters for retirement success, cutting through the noise and distractions. Ultimately, it's all about managing behavior, because even the best-laid financial plans can go awry when emotions take the driver's seat. As we dive deeper, we'll unpack how emotional control and behavioral discipline can make all the difference in reaching your retirement goals.

Behavioral economics is the study of how humans interact with money. Here, we will focus on one particular area of behavioral economics: investor behavior. Most of us would like to believe that we make rational decisions with our money, but research and statistics prove otherwise. We are highly emotional creatures, after all. We will make some mistakes. In this chapter, I want to give you insights into how we can identify common investing behavior problems and work to grow from our mistakes or, better yet, make fewer mistakes!

The Dalbar Report: Why We're Not as Good at Investing as We Think

The 30th annual DALBAR Quantitative Analysis of Investor Behavior (QAIB) report,[17] released in April 2024, highlights key insights into how investor behavior impacts returns. It shows that despite a robust market performance in 2023, investor behavior continues to detract from potential returns.

Key Findings:

1. **Equity Fund Investor Performance:** On average, equity fund investors earned 5.5 percent less than the S&P 500 in 2023. This represents the third-largest performance gap in the past decade.

---

[17] DALBAR, Inc. (2024, April 11). *DALBAR releases 30th annual QAIB report: Investor behavior continues to hinder returns*. DALBAR. https://www.dalbar.com

2. **Fixed Income Investor Performance:** Fixed income investors also underperformed, earning 2.63 percent less than the Bloomberg Barclays Aggregate Bond Index.

3. **Impact of Emotional Decisions:** The report emphasizes that emotional decision-making, such as selling investments during market downturns and missing subsequent rebounds, significantly harms investor returns.

4. **2022 versus 2023 Performance**: In 2022 the average equity fund investor had a return of -21.17 percent compared to the S&P 500's -18.11 percent. In 2023, despite improved market conditions, the performance gap widened with the average equity fund investor earning 20.79 percent against the S&P 500's 26.29 percent.

Unfortunately, it's not just less performance in the stock market years. It's also worse performance when the market is down (as was the case in 2022). Outside of hubris or great distrust for financial advisors, I cannot imagine why anyone would try and invest on their own.

Panic Selling and Poor Investment Choices

Based on this research, the two biggest ways that people lose in the market are:

1. *Panic Selling during Downturns:* Panic selling can occur for all sorts of reasons. We might start selling just because we do not like seeing our portfolio value decrease. We might sell because a trusted person advises us to. Or we might sell because a finance expert on TV tells us to. Whatever the reason, selling when the market dips is not advisable. We should be doing the opposite, but this is a difficult emotion to overcome.

2. *Choosing Investments without Enough Knowledge:* This happens because we are impatient and do not research enough. That's why I argue for keeping it simple and buying a basket of stocks in the form of an index fund instead of wasting time choosing individual stocks. Another reason for poor investment choices is ego. Many people think they can beat the market. They get overconfident in their abilities and end up losing. This leads to ego-driven investing, where market gains are attributed to skill and knowledge but losses are blamed on bad luck or external factors.

To eliminate both of these issues, stick to your 401(k) investing strategy and keep consistently pouring money into index funds. The beauty of the 401(k) lies in its simplicity—each paycheck automatically feeds your investments, allowing you to naturally dollar-cost average your way into the market without a second thought. There's zero emotion involved here—seriously, it's the ultimate "set it and forget it" approach! And remember, for the love of your future self, seek advice from a credentialed investment professional who acts as a fiduciary. That's someone who's legally obligated to put your best interests first, not just pad their own pocket. By following these strategies, you'll steer clear of the common DIY investing traps and ensure you don't miss out on those golden opportunities that pave the way to a secure retirement.

Prospect Theory: The Pain of Losing

An even more powerful emotion we need to understand when investing is called the "prospect theory." This theory coincides with feelings of loss aversion, fear of missing out (FOMO), and fear of regret. Prospect theory in finance describes the phenomenon where people feel stronger regret over losing money than pleasure from gaining the same amount. For example, someone may feel pleased if their portfolio increases by $20,000 in a week but feel significantly more distressed, relatively speaking, if it decreases by the same amount.

This is because we value things at a higher level than what the real market value might be. This same feeling leads to loss aversion. Because we do not want to experience the feeling of loss, we either do not invest at all in the stock market or we choose to invest in stocks that are increasing. Rational investing theories state that we should be *buying* when the market is low and selling when the market is high. But these theories are not human.

Fear of Missing Out (FOMO) and Media Bias

We all know FOMO can make us do crazy things, especially when it comes to investing. The constant pressure from news reports, social media, and those friends who won't stop bragging about their latest stock market wins can push us to make irrational investment choices. We don't want to miss out on the next Google or Amazon, so we dive in headfirst without thinking it through. Two prime examples of FOMO-driven investing are the cryptocurrency craze and the Reddit-fueled GameStop (GME) surge. But remember, most FOMO investing is pure speculation, not solid investing.

When we talk about media bias, we're looking at both corporate media giants like Fox News, CNN, and MSNBC and social media platforms like Reddit, Facebook, and Instagram. Media bias influences every aspect of our lives, but especially our investment decisions.

The media industry thrives on consumption. They make money from advertisers who pay top dollar to get their ads in front of large audiences. And what's the best way to attract more viewers? Bad news! According to Investor Place, nearly 90 percent of news articles in 2021 were negative. Sure, this was during the COVID-19 pandemic, but it highlights a larger trend: positive news doesn't sell as well, so media companies churn out the negative stuff.

You've probably heard doom-and-gloom phrases like "The market is tanking," "The Dow dropped more than 20 points this morning," or "The economy will decrease by 10 percent!" But guess what? None of this should worry you if you stick to the strategies laid out in this book. If it helps, consider deleting social media apps and blocking corporate news channels on your devices. After all, we don't let them dictate our diet choices, so why let them control our investing behavior?

Remember, stay cool, stick to your plan, and don't let FOMO or media hysteria derail your investment journey!

Combating Our Emotions

We could explore many more financial behaviors, but this is not a psychology book. If this content interests you, I suggest reading *Psychology of Money*, by Morgan Housel; *Thinking, Fast and Slow*, by Daniel Kahneman; or *Misbehaving: The Making of Behavioral Economics*, by Richard Thaler. There are dozens of great books about behavioral economics that can enrich your reading list, but these are a few of my favorites.

To make sure this brief discussion of behavioral economics enhances your retirement decision-making, let's discuss how we can rein in our emotions and take control of our investments. The first step is to identify your strongest biases. Again, this could be trust in social media, overconfidence, FOMO, loss aversion, or another behavior we did not mention. Once you identify your struggling area, take steps to eliminate that influence from your life.

The next step is to have a strong investment strategy that fits your lifestyle. I recommend the most basic one: invest in your employer's 401(k) plan and choose low-cost index funds. Stick with what you know in investments; do not invest outside of your skill and knowledge. Automate this process as much as you can. The more you automate your budgeting, saving, and investing process, the more emotions you take out of the equation. If you really need some more help, consider hiring a financial advisor who is credentialed and experienced and who is required to act as a fiduciary to give you the next level of expertise and comfort.

Another thought to comfort you—understand that the stock market is always going up. There are days, weeks, months, and even years when it goes down, but the stock market has historically trended positively. If the day comes when the stock market gets wiped out entirely, you do not need to worry about your investments. You'll need to worry about food and water instead because the world as we know it may be coming to an end.

Understanding Market History and Opportunity

Financial Crisis (2007–2009)
In 2009 the global economy was reeling from the aftermath of the 2008 financial crisis, one of the most severe economic downturns since the Great Depression. The crisis was triggered by the collapse of the housing bubble in the United States, leading to massive losses in mortgage-backed securities and the failure or near collapse of major financial institutions.

In September 2008 Lehman Brothers filed for the largest bankruptcy in US history and Merrill Lynch avoided a similar fate by selling to Bank of America. AIG required a $182 billion government bailout due to exposure to credit default swaps, while Citigroup faced severe liquidity issues and received multiple government bailouts. Washington Mutual, the largest US savings and loan association, was seized by regulators, and its assets were sold to JPMorgan Chase. These events highlighted the financial system's vulnerabilities and the widespread impact of the crisis.

A sharp contraction in economic activity, widespread job losses, and a severe liquidity crunch marked this period. Governments and central banks around the world implemented unprecedented measures to stabilize the financial system, including bailouts, monetary easing, and fiscal stimulus packages. Despite these efforts, consumer and business confidence was at an all-time low, and fears of a prolonged recession were widespread.

Investor Behavior

Investor behavior during this period was characterized by extreme caution and pessimism. Many investors, having suffered significant losses, withdrew from the stock market and sought safety in cash, government bonds, and other low-risk assets. The sentiment was dominated by fear and uncertainty, with many believing that the financial system's foundations were irreparably damaged. This resulted in a significant drop in stock prices, culminating in the S&P 500 hitting its low point on March 9, 2009 (676.53).

At the bottom, savvy investors who recognized the long-term value began cautiously reentering the market, capitalizing on undervalued stocks. This period also saw increased market volatility, with sharp swings driven by news of economic indicators, policy announcements, and corporate earnings reports. Despite the bleak outlook, the foundations for a recovery were laid, eventually leading to one of the longest bull markets in history.

Dollar-cost averaging (mentioned in the previous chapter) allowed diligent 401(k) investors who kept their jobs during the 2007–2009 financial crisis to steadily buy into the market as it declined, with each paycheck contributing to their investments. For those who stuck to their plan and didn't panic during the market lows in March 2009, the shares they acquired are now up over 700 percent, with annual returns exceeding 14 percent as of July 2024. This illustrates the power of behavioral discipline and the importance of managing emotions, especially in turbulent markets, whether through retirement accounts or taxable investments.

The Most Difficult Investing Time for Many

The stock market from 1999 to 2002 was like a roller-coaster ride, but without the fun and safety harnesses. This period was dominated by the rise and fall of the technology sector, often called the dot-com bubble. Imagine everyone throwing their money at any company with a ".com" in its name, hoping to strike it rich. It was the Wild West of investing, with valuations of tech stocks skyrocketing. The NASDAQ Composite index, packed with tech companies, nearly tripled from 1998 until it reached its peak in March 2000.

But, like all good parties, this one couldn't last. Many dot-com companies were all flash and no cash, lacking sustainable business models and failing to generate profits. By late 2000 reality hit hard and the bubble began to burst. The NASDAQ lost nearly 80 percent of its value from its peak, crashing from over 5,000 in March 2000 to around 1,100 by October 2002. The S&P 500 also took a nosedive, marking one of the most challenging periods in recent stock market history.

Investors made some classic blunders during this time. Remember Pets.com, with its sock puppet mascot? Many thought a company selling pet supplies online was a guaranteed winner. Spoiler alert: it wasn't. Or how about Webvan, which promised grocery deliveries but ended up delivering bankruptcy instead? These cautionary tales show the perils of jumping on the hype train without doing your homework.

The aftermath of the tech bubble burst led to what's often referred to as the "lost decade" for investors. From 2000 to 2010, the stock market delivered pretty disappointing returns. The S&P 500, for instance, ended the decade nearly flat when accounting for inflation, despite periods of recovery. The decade had its fair share of drama, too, including the 9/11 terrorist attacks in 2001, the accounting scandals of Enron and WorldCom, and the early 2000s recession.

S&P 500 Performance during the Dot-Com Bust
Let's break down the S&P 500's performance during those turbulent years:

- 2000: The S&P 500 declined by about 10.14 percent. This year marked the peak of the bubble and the beginning of its burst.

- 2001: The index continued its slide, falling by around 13.04 percent. This year was marred by the 9/11 attacks and a recession.

- 2002: The S&P 500 plummeted by approximately 23.37 percent, influenced by corporate scandals like Enron and WorldCom and ongoing economic struggles.

These three years of negative returns resulted in a cumulative loss of over 40 percent, reflecting the gut-wrenching volatility and uncertainty that defined this era. The experience was far worse for those invested in technology stocks and tech-focused mutual funds. This period underscores the importance of diversified investment strategies, dollar cost averaging, and the grand benefits of the 401(k) plan where investors systematically take a portion of their paycheck and invest in a mutual fund. Simultaneously, the volatility underscores the inherent risks of chasing speculative bubbles.

Conclusion

Not all market ups and downs will be this dramatic, but the point I want to emphasize here is that such volatility has emotional and psychological impact on all investors—so it's key we learn how to rein in our responses. The greatest challenges to investment success often come not from the market itself but from our own behaviors and emotions. These behavioral pitfalls, whether panic selling during downturns or the allure of chasing the next big thing, can derail even the best-laid plans,

But you can sidestep these common traps by embracing strategies like dollar-cost averaging, consistently investing in your 401(k) plan, and seeking wise investment and planning counsel. As you continue on your journey toward retirement success, remember that mastering your mindset is just as crucial as managing your money. The power to succeed is within your control—steady your hand, stay disciplined, and let your long-term strategy guide the way.

Key Points from Chapter 13

1. **Impact of Emotions on Investing:** Despite our belief in rational decision-making, emotions heavily influence our investment choices, often leading to poor outcomes.

2. **Dangers of Panic Selling:** Panic selling during market downturns is a common mistake that can severely impact long-term investment returns.

3. **Prospect Theory and Loss Aversion:** Losses are felt more intensely than gains, leading to irrational investment decisions driven by fear of loss.

4. **Influence of FOMO:** Fear of missing out, fueled by media and social pressure, can lead to impulsive and speculative investment decisions.

5. **Media Bias and Negative News:** The media often focuses on negative news, which can exacerbate fear and lead to poor investment decisions. Recognizing this bias is crucial.

6. **Benefits of Dollar-Cost Averaging:** Regular, automated investing in low-cost index funds through strategies like dollar-cost averaging helps mitigate emotional decision-making and promotes long-term growth.

7. **Historical Market Trends for Long-Term Growth:** The stock market has historically trended upward over long periods. Understanding this can help investors stay calm during market dips and avoid panic selling.

CHAPTER 14

FROM PEN TO PLATFORM: BRIDGING THEORY AND REALITY IN FINANCIAL LITERACY

Given the abundance of advice, statistics, and prognostications on retirement, it's crucial for you to understand the relationship between theory and actions that will ensure success in your own planning process. That's what we'll accomplish in this penultimate chapter.

The Joy of Writing and Research

As an extreme introvert, writing is my happy place. Research feeds my soul. Despite the challenges, writing my dissertation was a joy. Every night, after the kids went to bed, I'd retreat to my home office and dive headfirst into academic theory surrounding financial literacy and behavior. It was like a nightly getaway, but instead of sandy beaches, there were stacks of research papers and data spreadsheets.

While theoretical concepts are all about the what-ifs, applied theory is where the rubber meets the road. It's about taking those brainy theories and making them work in the real world. In financial literacy, applied theory turns academic insights into practical tools and strategies that help people get a grip on their finances and make smarter money moves.

From Research to Real Life with DocMoneyFish

In my postdoctoral work, I've pondered the anonymous heroes who filled out my dissertation surveys. It's funny how you can feel a connection to a bunch of data points without ever meeting the people behind them. So I wanted to change the lack of engagement with the survey respondents and bring their stories to life.

At the same time, I research financial literacy and behavior each day. I also listen to financial media such as Bloomberg and CNBC. I read and hear some of the craziest things. For example, in May 2024, a Harris poll was conducted showing nearly 50 percent of respondents thought the S&P 500 Index was down for the year (when the S&P was up over 12 percent). This is meaningful as it may explain why so many people fail to save for retirement, given the stock market is a primary savings tool for individuals looking to invest for their future.

So I created a platform (called DocMoneyFish, or DMF) to share information bidirectionally. In one direction, I will highlight interviews with individuals so we can all hear and learn about other people's views on money. How are they using money, thinking about money, spending money, et cetera? Importantly, this platform is aimed at financial services firms, universities, and governments so they can hear what people are saying and doing with their money. It is essential that these groups get out from behind the computer, the spreadsheets, and the data, and see their respondents face-to-face.

In the other direction, I'll share financial knowledge that can benefit those I'm interviewing and help dispel common myths and misconceptions about spending, saving, borrowing, and investing. For example, individuals need to know that the stock market has a tremendous track record in making people money. Importantly, more people need to save for retirement and at the same time know that Social Security is not the retirement most people hope for. This is real and true and important for individuals to know. Either way, in both directions, I want to use real stories and solid research to do my work.

The Declining Knowledge Paradox is Real

Individual financial knowledge is on the decline.[18] Even though we're throwing hundreds of millions of dollars at

---

18 Urban, C., & Valdes, O. (2022). *Why is measured financial literacy declining and what does it mean? Maybe We just "don't know."* Insights: Financial Capability. FINRA Investor Education Foundation.

financial education, it's not working.[19] Yep, you heard that right—the more we spend trying to teach people about money, the less they seem to know. It's like a bizarre financial Twilight Zone.

And it's not just that financial knowledge is on the decline (and has been in every survey since 2009). The decrease in financial knowledge has coincided with poor financial behavior, including general anxiety around money, a lack of emergency savings, and a staggering number of individuals who have saved poorly for retirement. Why do only 50 percent of individuals pay off their credit cards each year, on average? Why have over 25 percent of people aged 18 to 34 taken hardship loans from their retirement accounts? And why do only 43 percent of individuals in the same age group have a retirement account?

We hope to explore financial knowledge, savings, investing, and borrowing trends through our DocMoneyFish platform.

Food for Thought: Speaking Their Language

There are a host of reasons the US consumer has low financial acuity and poor financial behavior. At the top of the list is the way we talk about money. After conducting a dozen interviews on the street, I learned quickly that there is a definition gap between everyday Americans and those

---

19 Consumer Financial Protection Bureau. (2022). *Financial literacy annual report: Fiscal year 2021.* https://files.consumerfinance.gov/f/documents/cfpb_financial-literacy-fy-2021_annual-report_2022-03.pdf

charged with teaching, researching, and developing policy around financial education.

This definition—divide is real. Take, for example, the topic of inflation. When asking individuals about inflation, I assumed those I was speaking with knew little—and their responses confirmed my assumption. But what I found is that instead of asking someone about inflation, I should ask them to talk about their grocery bill, water bill, gas prices, or if baby formula was getting more expensive or less. Or better yet, ask if they've experienced sticker shock, dollar shrink, money meltdown, or cost creep.

And when it comes to money, don't assume everyone wants to discuss it in dry, boring terms. If you ask if you can "hit them up," "rap," or "chop it up" about scrilla, paper, or racks, they'll likely want to tell you their story or at a minimum, be open to answering a few questions. After all, are we trying to sound smart, or do we want to learn about whether individuals understand financial concepts? The bottom line? **Whether it's someone on the street or a 401(k) investor, we can't expect them to speak our language. Out of respect, we need to learn theirs.**

An Education in Los Angeles

Picture this: I flew to LAX for my first filming adventure. My son Owen, fresh out of film school and full of big ideas, suggested Santa Monica. It's close to his place in LA and brimming with beachgoers soaking up the sun—perfect for interviews, right? He nailed it. But what I discovered was mind-blowing. Only 10 percent of the people I talked to had a 401(k), were invested in the stock market, or had a traditional savings account earning interest. In my view, these individuals were not financially illiterate; they just thought about saving and investing differently than many of us do.

Turns out, the classic approach of saving for retirement, investing in stocks, and stashing cash in a savings account is either out of reach, boring, or just plain sketchy to most folks. Instead, the majority were all about cryptocurrency (like Bitcoin and Ethereum), hard assets like real estate and precious metals, and good old-fashioned cash. These people had street smarts, even if their financial IQ wasn't textbook.

Take one guy I interviewed, who retired at 43. Yeah, you read that right—43! He was previously incarcerated, but when he got out, he landed a construction job doing work on an Ivy League campus. Fast-forward a few years, and he got some shares in the company. When he sold those shares, he cashed in big-time. He invested in real estate and time-shares, managing short-term rentals for passive income. This guy's life now? Traveling the country with his daughter and wife or chilling in LA.

I asked if he ever thought about the stock market. His response? A hard no. He'd seen too many people lose their shirts in stocks and didn't trust "the system." For him, the racks he's made in real estate—thanks to cash flow and appreciation—are more than enough. He doesn't think he could've hit the same jackpot with traditional investments.

So what's the takeaway? People aren't clueless about finances; they just have different strategies. And honestly, who can blame them? Whether it's crypto, real estate, or plain cash, they're finding their own paths to financial freedom.

New Types of Assets

It is clear that Gen Z and millennials are taking a different approach to retirement savings. A 2024 study by Bank of America highlights that younger investors prefer crypto, private equity, direct investments, and real estate over stocks and bonds.[20] Alternative assets might be the knight in shining armor for the next generation. We're talking about cryptocurrencies like Bitcoin and Ethereum, tangible assets like real estate and precious metals, and yes, even plain old cash. These aren't just buzzwords; the next generation views these assets as game-changers. Traditional investments like stocks, bonds, and interest-bearing savings accounts—along with 401(k)s and IRAs—have been the bread and butter for decades. But for many young folks, they're about as exciting as a root canal.

Novel investment approaches are driven by the ability to make more quickly, which can accelerate becoming financially independent early (remember FIRE) or provide an oversize asset pool to live off during retirement.

Cryptocurrency: The Digital Gold Rush

Cryptocurrencies have taken the world by storm. Bitcoin, Ethereum, and their digital buddies offer something the

---

20 Bank of America Private Bank (2024). *2024 Bank of America Private Bank study of wealthy Americans*. https://www.privatebank.bankofamerica.com/articles/generational-divide-wealth-study.html

stock market doesn't: decentralization. There's no middleman skimming off the top, and transactions are lightning fast. Plus, the potential for high returns is like a siren call for young investors. Sure, it's volatile, but for a generation that grew up with the internet and rapid change, that's just part of the thrill. Compare that to the stock market, which can feel like watching paint dry, and it's easy to see why crypto is winning hearts and wallets.

Real Estate: Bricks, Mortar, and Big Returns
Real estate is another hot favorite. It's tangible, it's relatable, and it's a proven wealth builder. Whether it's buying a home, investing in rental properties, or dabbling in real estate crowdfunding, there's something inherently satisfying about owning a piece of the earth. Plus, real estate offers multiple income streams—rent payments, property appreciation, and tax benefits. Contrast this with the often abstract nature of stocks and bonds, and you'll understand why real estate feels like a safer bet. It's a lot harder for a house to vanish into thin air than a stock's value.

Precious Metals: Solid and Secure
Then there's the allure of precious metals like gold and silver. They've been around since ancient times, and they're not going anywhere. Many feel these metals hedge against inflation and economic downturns, offering a sense of security that's hard to beat. Young investors, wary of market crashes and economic instability, find comfort in the steady, shiny allure of precious metals.

Cash: King of Flexibility

Let's not forget cash. It's liquid, it's versatile, and it's straightforward. In a world where financial systems can feel like a labyrinth, cash is the simplest player on the board. It's immediate, it's tangible, and it doesn't require deciphering complex market trends or interest rates. For many young people, cash is not just king—it's a lifesaver.

Traditional Investments: The Old Guard

On the flip side, traditional investments like stocks, bonds, and mutual funds have their merits, no doubt. They offer familiarity, long-term growth, and in the case of 401(k)s and IRAs, significant tax advantages. But for a generation that values flexibility and immediate results, and distrusts traditional financial systems, these old-school methods can seem stifling.

The Bottom Line

Ultimately, the shift toward alternative assets is about more than just money—it's about mindset. Young investors are looking for control, excitement, and tangible results. Whether it's the digital allure of crypto, the solid foundation of real estate, the timeless value of precious metals, or the straightforward nature of cash, they're carving out their own paths to financial freedom.[21] And honestly? It's about time the financial world caught up. These individuals may be

---

21 Schultz, A. (2024, June 18). *Crypto, private equity, and hard assets are preferred by wealthy younger investors*. Penta. https://www.barrons.com/articles/younger-investors-prefer-crypto-private-equity-and-hard-assets-to-u-s-stocks-study-finds-e3fffce

unable to score well on a basic financial literacy assessment, but that's not surprising, given the types of questions we ask them. However, if asked about crypto, real estate, or getting by day to day, I think they'd ace that exam.

New Investors and New Accounts

What shocked me more than a cat on a Roomba was how the young people I interviewed (mostly under 30) viewed investment accounts—especially retirement vehicles like 401(k)s and IRAs. Most of them either had no clue what a 401(k) was, didn't have one, or once had one and ditched it. The lack of retirement accounts is consistent with US government studies and the Financial Capability Study sponsored by FINRA Investor Education Foundation.

Why Millennials and Gen Z Are Ditching Traditional Investments
Our beloved millennials and Gen Zers are veering away from traditional retirement accounts for many reasons, and the reasons are as varied as TikTok trends. Economic hurdles, social shifts, technological advancements, and a whole new attitude toward work and financial security are driving this change.

Living in the Now: The Long-Game Rejection
Many young folks I chatted with plan to work until they're ancient—or at least that's the vibe. Retirement isn't even on their radar. Instead, they're focused on the now, choosing to savor life and share their experiences instead of hoarding cash for a future that seems as distant as flying cars.

Economic Challenges: The Gig Economy Effect

Economic challenges play a huge role in this mindset. With the rise of freelance and gig work, fewer young adults have access to cushy, employer-sponsored retirement plans like 401(k)s. Frequent job changes and unstable employment mean they need savings that are more liquid and flexible—like a ninja's bank account.

The Student Loan Stranglehold

Debt is practically a rite of passage for those under 30, mostly in the form of student loans. It's no surprise they're prioritizing paying off this mountain of debt over contributing to retirement accounts. High monthly payments leave little room for anything else, making retirement savings feel like a pipe dream.

Mistrust in Traditional Financial Systems

There's also a massive trust issue. Many young people got front-row seats to the 2008 financial crisis. Whether they were young adults or just kids watching their parents liquidate everything, the aftermath of the "Great Recession" left a sour taste. Stories of corporate scandals and economic instability have fueled their distrust of the stock market and traditional financial institutions.

Craving Control and Flexibility

Unlike previous generations, who signed up for their 401(k) on their first day at the corporate gig, today's young investors want more control and flexibility over their finances. Investment accounts that lock up their money for 30-plus years (with penalties for early withdrawal) are about as appealing as a soggy sandwich. They prefer accounts they can liquidate easily and manage through slick apps.

Tech-Savvy Financial Revolution
Technology has flipped the financial world on its head, especially for digital natives like millennials and Gen Zers. Apps like Robinhood, Acorns, and Coinbase are their jam. Neobanks like Chime, Varo, and Current are replacing their parents' stodgy banks. Checks are as dead as disco, and even credit cards are losing their luster. Payment apps like Venmo, Cash App, and PayPal make transferring funds a breeze.

A New Financial Ecosystem
Budgeting tools like Mint and YNAB are the cherry on top of this new financial sundae. Together, these apps and platforms create a financial ecosystem that's second nature to them but utterly foreign to older generations. Welcome to the future of finance, where old-school methods are out and digital dominance is in.

The Bottom Line
Changing cultural attitudes and generational values are playing a significant role in the financial lives of those I interviewed—most of whom were between the ages of 18 and 34. It is crystal clear to me that they value experiences over assets, as these young people prioritize their quality of life and a stress-free approach to their day over long-term financial assets. Given modern life's fast-paced, uncertain

nature, planning for 30 to 40 years into the future seems less practical or relevant.

Unaffordable housing, health care expenses that have soared through the roof, and other inflationary pressures at the gas pump and grocery store have changed the priorities for those I interviewed. They are focused on paying their bills and if possible, prioritizing travel, education, starting a business, or developing their personal brand.

It is clear to me that traditional financial education regularly fails to address the realities and preferences of the younger generation. Counsel that emphasizes traditional retirement savings may not resonate with their current financial challenges and aspirations. To those that I interviewed or that have been nodding your head in agreement while you read, *I hear you*.

Conclusion

DocMoneyFish (DMF) is here to listen to your story, share your journey, and help you make smart and safe money moves. DMF is also about managing misconceptions about the financial system, answering questions about who you can trust, and the importance of saving for retirement. We get it—there's a lot of distrust in the system, and focusing on short-term needs is more important than ever. At the same time, if you can't or don't want to work forever, we need to make sure you have a plan that works for when you decide to kick back and relax. Let's ensure your approach is solid for both now and the future.

As I write this penultimate chapter, I want you to know you're not alone. It's not you; it's them. The previous generation might have their heads buried in the sand, but you? You're not financially illiterate. You prioritize the short term because, for some of you, it's a necessity, and for others, it's about living the retirement dream now, not decades later.

DMF exists to amplify your voice and learn your language. We aim to create awareness among lawmakers, academics, and older generations. You're not crazy—you just see things differently, and that demands a new, maybe even better, way of thinking. Let's make your financial future as bright as your present.

Key Points from Chapter 14

1. **Your Past Doesn't Need to Dictate Your Future:** If you've had a slow start or bumps along your way, having lasting financial success is still possible.

2. **Empowering Action through Practical Knowledge:** By applying financial literacy concepts to real-life scenarios, individuals can make smarter and more confident money decisions.

3. **Connecting Data with Real Stories**: The creation of the DocMoneyFish (DMF) platform aims to bridge the gap between data and the real-life stories behind it, enhancing engagement with survey respondents.

4. **Bilateral Information Exchange**: DMF facilitates a two-way exchange of information, sharing financial knowledge and collecting insights from diverse individuals about their financial experiences.

5. **Declining Financial Literacy**: Despite increased investment in financial education, overall financial literacy has declined, coinciding with poor financial behaviors and lack of savings.

6. **Understanding the Communication Gap**: There is a significant gap in how financial concepts are communicated and understood, highlighting the importance of using relatable language when discussing money matters.

7. **Changing Investment Trends**: Younger generations favor alternative assets like cryptocurrencies and real estate over traditional investments, driven by a desire for control and distrust of conventional financial systems.

CHAPTER 15

THE GRAND FINALE: YOUR JOURNEY TO 401(K) SUCCESS

As we reach the final chapter of *Becoming a 401(k) Millionaire*, it's time to reflect on the invaluable lessons we've explored together. We've delved into the intricacies of 401(k) plans, explored alternative savings strategies, and shared inspiring stories of individuals who have achieved financial success. We've also gone beyond the standard terrain of retirement planning, considering the emotional side of the process and mapping out today's expanded field of investing. Now let's tie it all together with a bang and leave you with the motivation to start—or enhance—your 401(k) journey.

The Big Picture: Your Financial Future Starts Now

The world of 401(k) investing might seem daunting, but as we've learned, it's one of the most powerful tools you have to secure a comfortable retirement. Whether you're just starting out or already on your way, the time to take action is now. Remember, the best time to plant a tree was 20 years ago; the second-best time is today. So let's get planting!

Key Takeaways from Our Journey

Chapter 1: From Small Beginnings to Big Dreams: The Power of a 401(k)

- Start early and invest consistently in a 401(k) to harness the power of compounding. Even small contributions can lead to significant wealth over time, especially with employer matching and low-cost investments.

Chapter 2: Your Retirement Road Trip: From Point A to 401(k)

- Prioritize working for companies with strong 401(k) plans, including employer matching and low-cost investment options. Understanding these benefits and committing to saving through your 401(k) is crucial for a secure financial future.

Chapter 3: Navigating Your Path to a Million-Dollar Retirement

- Be mindful of fees in your 401(k), and choose low-cost, diversified funds like target date or index funds to maximize growth. Consistency, emotional discipline, and understanding your investment options are key to reaching your retirement goals.

Chapter 4: The Power of Starting Early: Budgeting and Saving for Retirement

- Start saving for retirement as early as possible to take advantage of compounding. Maintain a budget, prioritize retirement contributions, and invest in low-cost index funds to maximize your savings potential over time. Stay committed to your investment strategy even during economic uncertainties.

Chapter 5: The Power of Small Decisions

- Small, consistent financial sacrifices, like skipping minor expenses, can accumulate into significant wealth over time when the leftover money is invested, highlighting the importance of mindful spending and saving.

Chapter 6: The Power of the 401(k) and the Reality of Social Security

- Relying solely on Social Security is risky due to potential future shortfalls; a 401(k) offers a more secure, tax-advantaged path to retirement savings and financial independence.

Chapter 7: Flipping the Switch: From Saver to Spender in Retirement

- Successfully transitioning to retirement involves careful planning, including assembling a trusted team of advisors, understanding investment strategies, and maximizing resources like Social Security.

Chapter 8: Tailored Retirement Solutions for Unique Situations

- There are diverse retirement savings options beyond the traditional 401(k), such as IRAs and plans for the self-employed, allowing tailored strategies for different employment and income situations.

Chapter 9: Financial Independence, Retire Early (FIRE): A Radical Approach

- The FIRE movement advocates extreme saving and investing to achieve financial independence and early retirement, challenging traditional work and retirement norms.

Chapter 10: The Late Bloomers: It's Never Too Late to Start Saving

- It's never too late to start saving for retirement; taking action now, regardless of your age, can significantly improve your financial future.

Chapter 11: Inspiring Savers: Real Stories of Hope

- Real-life examples show that consistent saving and investing through retirement accounts like a 401(k) can lead to financial success, regardless of one's starting point.

Chapter 12: Market Timing, the News, and Your Emotions

- Avoid trying to time the market; instead, focus on consistent investing through strategies like dollar-cost averaging to build wealth over the long term.

Chapter 13: Mastering the Mind: Navigating Investor Behavior and Emotions

- Managing emotions and avoiding impulsive investment decisions are crucial for achieving long-term financial success.

Chapter 14: From Pen to Platform: Bridging Theory and Reality in Financial Literacy

- Connecting real-life stories with financial literacy can bridge the gap between theory and practice, making financial education more relevant and accessible to all.

The Final Push: Get Started or Level Up

So here we are, standing at the precipice of your financial future. Whether you're a 401(k) newbie or a seasoned saver, there's always room for improvement. The key is to start now or take your current efforts to the next level. Here are a few final pieces of advice:

1. **Automate Your Savings:** Set up automatic contributions to your 401(k) or other retirement accounts. It's the easiest way to stay consistent.

2. **Increase Contributions Gradually:** If you can't max out your contributions right away, start with what you can afford and increase it annually.

3. **Educate Yourself:** The financial world is constantly evolving. Stay informed and be proactive about learning new investment strategies.

4. **Seek Professional Advice:** Don't hesitate to consult with a financial advisor. A little expert guidance can go a long way.

5. **Stay the Course:** Remember, investing is a marathon, not a sprint. Stay focused on your long-term goals and don't get sidetracked by short-term market fluctuations.

Going Out Strong

As we wrap up, let's go out strong—with lots of positive momentum! Becoming a 401(k) millionaire isn't just a dream; it's an achievable goal with the right mindset and actions. This book has equipped you with the knowledge, tools, and insight you need to make it happen. Now it's up to you to take the next steps.

Whether you're starting from scratch or refining your existing plan, the journey to financial freedom begins with a single step. So lace up those metaphorical sneakers, and let's hit the ground running. Your future self will thank you.

Cheers to your journey, your success, and your bright future. You've got this—now go out there and make your financial dreams a reality!

AUTHOR'S NOTE

Thank you for reading my book. I hope you've learned, or at least been reminded of, a thing or two that can benefit you or someone you know. If you've learned even one good thing from what I've shared, please pass it along to a friend, coworker, neighbor, or family member. Continue to make smart money moves by following me on most major social platforms on the handle @docmoneyfish, and feel free to email me anytime at docmoneyfish@gmail.com with feedback, questions, and comments.

APPENDIX

Chapter 1 Chart: 401(k) Savings Over Time

Key inputs used to generate the 401(k) savings over time chart:

1. Initial Salary: $40,000 per year

2. Annual Salary Increase: 2.1%

3. Employee 401(k) Contribution Rate: 6% of salary

4. Company Match Rate: 4% of salary

5. Annual Market Return Rate: 9%

6. Time Period: 40 years

401(k) Balance Growth:

- **10 Years:** The ending balance is approximately $73,313.

- **20 Years:** The ending balance is approximately $263,807.

- **30 Years:** The ending balance is approximately $735,622.

- **40 Years:** The ending balance is approximately $1,878,243.

Essential Lessons from the Chart:

1. **Impact of Time:** The chart illustrates the exponential growth of the 401(k) balance over time, demonstrating the power of compounding interest. The most significant growth occurs in the latter years,

emphasizing the importance of early and consistent contributions.

2. **Importance of Contributions:** Employee contributions and company match collectively enhance the growth, leading to a substantial retirement fund.

Other Notes to Consider:

To provide an estimate, I assume a 9 percent average rate of return, assuming an individual is consistently invested in equities (stocks). This may appear too low for some and too high for others. But it's just a number. Get over it.

Returns vary over time. Past returns are just that—in the past. Although we are all hopeful of favorable future returns, there is no guarantee the past will repeat itself. That said, below are the average returns of the S&P 500 over 10, 20, 30, and 40 years.

- **Last 10 Years**: The S&P 500 had an average annual return of approximately 11.8 percent (Investopedia, YCharts).

- **Last 20 Years**: The average annual return was around 7.6 percent (Investopedia, YCharts).

- **Last 30 Years**: The average annual return was about 9.7 percent (Investopedia, YCharts).

- **Last 40 Years**: The average annual return was approximately 10.26 percent (Investopedia, YCharts).

Wage growth has averaged above 2.6 percent in the last ten years and over 3 percent for 20-, 30-, and 40-year periods. To provide a conservative estimate, I assumed wages increase at 2.1 percent. Again, this number is not gospel, but let's focus on the data.

- **Last 10 Years:** Wage growth has averaged around 2.6 percent per year.

- **Last 20 Years:** The average annual wage growth was approximately 3.1 percent.

- **Last 30 Years:** The average annual wage growth was about 3.3 percent.

- **Last 40 Years:** Wage growth over this period averaged around 3.5 percent.

For your reference, here are some additional market return scenarios:

- 7 percent Annual Return:

    - 10 Years: The ending balance is approximately $65,651.

    - 20 Years: The ending balance is approximately $209,962.

- 30 Years: The ending balance is approximately $512,511.

- 40 Years: The ending balance is approximately $1,130,653.

- 9 percent Annual Return:

  - 10 Years: The ending balance is approximately $73,313.

  - 20 Years: The ending balance is approximately $263,807.

  - 30 Years: The ending balance is approximately $735,622.

  - 40 Years: The ending balance is approximately $1,878,243.

- 11 percent Annual Return:

  - 10 Years: The ending balance is approximately $81,925.

  - 20 Years: The ending balance is approximately $333,471.

  - 30 Years: The ending balance is approximately $1,071,011.

- 40 Years: The ending balance is approximately $3,193,874.

Chapter 2 Chart: 401(k) Savings Over Time with Auto Escalation

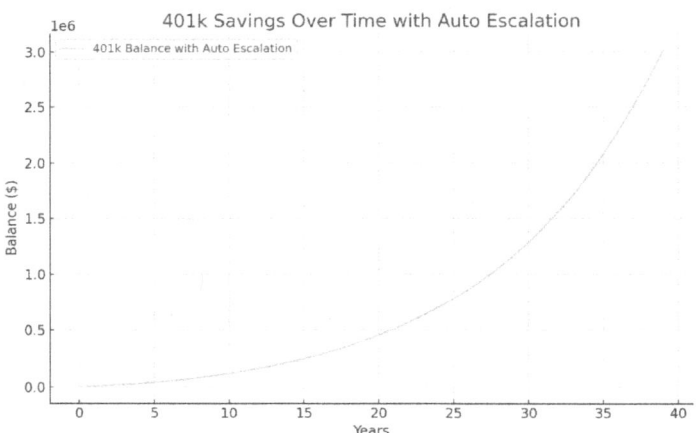

Key inputs for the chart on 401(k) savings over time with auto escalation:

1. Initial Salary: $40,000 per year

2. Annual Salary Increase: 2.1 percent

3. Employee 401(k) Contribution Rate: Starts at 6 percent of salary

4. Auto Escalation: Employee contribution increases by 1 percent per year for 9 years, capping at 15 percent

5. Company Match Rate: 4 percent of salary

6. Annual Market Return Rate: 9 percent

7. Time Period: 40 years

Observations

1. **Increasing Contributions:** The employee's contribution starts at 6 percent and increases by 1 percent each year until it reaches 15 percent in the 10th year. This results in a higher contribution amount over time compared to a fixed contribution rate.

2. **Growth of 401(k) Balance:** The 401(k) balance grows significantly over the 40-year period due to the combination of increasing contributions, company match, salary increases, and market returns. The growth is exponential, reflecting the impact of compound interest over a long period.

3. **Impact of Auto Escalation:** The auto-escalation feature leads to a steeper increase in the 401(k) balance in the early years, which compounds over time. This strategy effectively leverages the power

of compounding, resulting in a significantly higher final balance compared to a fixed contribution rate.

4. **Long-Term Benefits:** By the end of the 40-year period, the balance is considerably higher, showcasing the benefits of both consistent contributions and market performance. The employee's proactive approach to increasing their contribution rate plays a crucial role in maximizing their retirement savings.

Chapter 6 Notes on Social Security: Key Dates in the History of Social Security

- **1935:** President Franklin D. Roosevelt signs the Social Security Act into law.

- **1937:** Collection of Social Security taxes begins.

- **1940:** The first monthly retirement check is issued.

- **1954:** Amendments to the act expand coverage to more workers.

- **1956:** Disability Insurance Program is established.

- **1965:** Medicare and Medicaid are established as part of the Social Security Act.

- **1972:** The Supplemental Security Income (SSI) program is created.

- **1983:** Significant amendments are enacted to ensure solvency, including a gradual increase in retirement age.

- **2000:** Elimination of the earnings limit for older workers, for work in retirement, without retirement benefits being withheld.

- **2024:** The fund that assists in paying for Social Security benefits is due to run out by 2035—with retirees scheduled to receive 83 percent of the scheduled benefit at that time.

Chapter 9 Chart: FIRE Movement Savings Example

Year	Portfolio Value
0	0.00
1	$26,705.00
2	$55,615.95
3	$87,063.38
4	$121,412.09
5	$159,065.22
6	$200,468.09
7	$246,112.22
8	$296,541.32
9	$352,355.04

10	$ 414,214.00
11	$ 482,847.26
12	$ 559,057.11
13	$ 643,728.26
14	$ 737,836.80
15	$ 842,458.58
16	$ 958,779.85
17	$ 1,088,107.02
18	$ 1,231,877.64
19	$ 1,391,685.64
20	$ 1,569,296.35
21	$ 1,766,668.01
22	$ 1,986,980.14
23	$ 2,232,645.96

In this table, we assume the following:

Annual Salary:

- The individual earns an annual salary of $50,000.

Employee Contribution Rate:

- The employee contributes 20 percent of their annual salary to their 401(k) plan. This is the maximum personal contribution rate allowable under IRS guidelines for 2024.

Employer Match Rate:

- The employer matches 4 percent of the employee's annual salary in contributions to the 401(k) plan.

Annual Contribution Limit:

- The maximum annual contribution limit for 401(k) plans in 2024 is $22,500. This is the maximum amount the employee can defer from their salary.

Total Annual Contribution:

- The total annual contribution to the 401(k) plan is the sum of the employee's contribution and the employer's match. In this case, it is $22,500 (employee) + $2,000 (employer) = $24,500 per year.

Annual Return Rate:

- The investment in the 401(k) plan is assumed to earn an average annual return of 9 percent, which is typical for a diversified portfolio invested primarily in the S&P 500 index.

Target Portfolio Value:

- The goal is to accumulate a portfolio value of $2,000,000.

Timeframe:

- The time required to reach the target portfolio value of $2,000,000 is approximately 23 years, given the annual contributions and the assumed rate of return.

www.ingramcontent.com/pod-product-compliance
Lightning Source LLC
Chambersburg PA
CBHW052146220526
45471CB00004B/1550